Mimi Dietrich's

BALTIMORE BASICS
Album Quilts from Start to Finish

Martingale®
& COMPANY

Mimi Dietrich's Baltimore Basics:
Album Quilts from Start to Finish
© 2006 by Mimi Dietrich

That Patchwork Place® is an imprint of
Martingale & Company®.

Martingale & Company
20205 144th Avenue NE
Woodinville, WA 98072-8478 USA
www.martingale-pub.com

Credits

President • Nancy J. Martin
CEO • Daniel J. Martin
COO • Tom Wierzbicki
Publisher • Jane Hamada
Editorial Director • Mary V. Green
Managing Editor • Tina Cook
Technical Editor • Cyndi Hershey
Copy Editor • Melissa Bryan
Design Director • Stan Green
Illustrator • Laurel Strand
Cover and Text Designer • Shelly Garrison
Photographer • Brent Kane

Printed in China
11 10 09 08 07 06   8 7 6 5 4 3 2 1

Library of Congress Cataloging-In-Publication Data

Library of Congress Control Number: 2006014376

ISBN-13: 978-1-56477-678-5
ISBN-10: 1-56477-678-6

Mission Statement

Dedicated to providing quality products and service to inspire creativity.

Dedication

To all my students who have shared the Baltimore appliqué journey with me.

Acknowledgments

Many, many thanks to:

Cyndi Hershey for planting the seed that started this project.

The students in my Baltimore Album, Grad School, and PHD classes.

Karan Flanscha for her Baltimore Blue Work quilt.

Robbyn Robinson for color suggestions.

Libbie Rollman for her quilting tips.

Annette Dietrich for her "envelope" label idea.

Barbara Burnham for her expert appliqué tips.

Norma Campbell and Linda Newson for listening.

Penny Clifton for finishing her quilt.

"Monday Night Madness," consisting of Laurie Gregg, Joan Costello, and Barbara McMahon for living with my appliqué blocks on our retreat.

"Baltimore or Bust," a group of ladies who are determined to finish their quilts by helping each other: Dianna Storck, Trisha Raidt, Nora Reedy, Cheryl Travis, Lilllian Lowery, Carol Paull, Millie Lorenz, Jean Berk, Kathy Smith, Kathy Ockuly, Joan Hayden, and Joan Hopkins.

Karen Soltys, Mary Green, Nancy Martin, Terry Martin, and everyone at Martingale who makes my dreams come true.

And Bob Dietrich, a great quilter's husband.
Thanks, Hon!

Contents

Introduction • 4

Planning Your Quilt • 6

Designing Your Quilt • 8

Appliqué Fabrics • 19

Determining Yardage and Cutting • 21

Appliqué Supplies • 30

Getting Ready to Appliqué • 32

Preparing Appliqué Pieces • 38

Hand-Basting Primer • 41

Hand-Appliqué Stitch Techniques • 46

Elements of Baltimore-Style Appliqué • 50

Baltimore Basic Dimensional Techniques • 59

Using the Block Lessons • 62

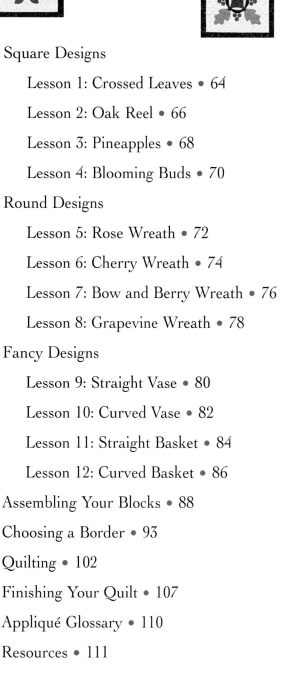

Square Designs

    Lesson 1: Crossed Leaves • 64

    Lesson 2: Oak Reel • 66

    Lesson 3: Pineapples • 68

    Lesson 4: Blooming Buds • 70

Round Designs

    Lesson 5: Rose Wreath • 72

    Lesson 6: Cherry Wreath • 74

    Lesson 7: Bow and Berry Wreath • 76

    Lesson 8: Grapevine Wreath • 78

Fancy Designs

    Lesson 9: Straight Vase • 80

    Lesson 10: Curved Vase • 82

    Lesson 11: Straight Basket • 84

    Lesson 12: Curved Basket • 86

Assembling Your Blocks • 88

Choosing a Border • 93

Quilting • 102

Finishing Your Quilt • 107

Appliqué Glossary • 110

Resources • 111

About the Author • 112

Introduction

Welcome to Baltimore! You're about to begin a wonderful journey as you appliqué designs inspired by quilts made in Baltimore more than 150 years ago. This is your guidebook!

I've lived my entire life in Baltimore, Maryland. Twenty-five years ago I saw an exhibit of antique album quilts at the Baltimore Museum of Art and I was inspired! I could not believe the wonderful colors, small appliqué stitches, and beautiful quilting designs—all created by women in my hometown nearly 150 years before. That exhibit greatly influenced my life as a quilter. I love appliqué!

I've taught Baltimore Album appliqué classes in the Baltimore area for 20 years. My first students made quilts using a pattern with four small blocks adapted from the antique quilts. Since 1990, I've taught a yearlong class using designs from Elly Sienkiewicz, Jeana Kimball, and a variety of other sources, including *Baltimore Bouquets*, my book of 10" block designs featuring dimensional appliqué techniques.

I've had some great experiences with the museums in Baltimore that collect these antique quilts. A visit with friends to the Maryland Historical Society led to the creation of a special guild in Baltimore called the Baltimore Appliqué Society. This group has helped the Historical Society and the Baltimore Museum of Art by preparing exhibits, demonstrating appliqué techniques, and acting as docents during exhibits. The members made quilts to benefit the collections and even had quilts on display in the museums. Studying the old quilts is a wonderful inspiration when making a Baltimore quilt.

I am always thrilled to see a student finish a quilt! I know the time it takes to appliqué the blocks. In addition, there are so many other decisions to make about colors, settings, and quilting designs. It is truly an accomplishment when a quilt is completed.

I have a group of students who meet once a month called my "Graduate Students." We have show-and-tell and always take time to celebrate a finished quilt with "oohs," "aahs," and questions about designs and techniques. We even have a "PHD" program in which the projects just get "Piled Higher and Deeper."

Each quilt tells a story through the variety of blocks in the album. These blocks evoke memories of family and friends, special occasions and places, and historical events. One of my favorite stories comes from a student who told us that she felt the presence of her grandmother as she stitched a block. Many students have included yellow ribbon and patriotic designs to provide subtle stitching clues

about the quilt's date for future quilt historians.

I've made several small Baltimore-style quilts and, at this writing, have almost finished my second full-size quilt. After the last class show-and-tell, I realized that I enjoy making these quilts, but it's truly my passion to be involved with students making these quilts *in Baltimore*. I love to inspire quilters, to help them choose colors, learn appliqué techniques, gain confidence, get excited about the process, and, in a sense, repeat history. I have had the very special opportunity of connecting quilters here in Baltimore with quilts that were made long ago in our city.

I love to inspire quilters to put their blocks together and *finish* their quilts. The following pages offer tips from my classes and suggestions from my students. More than 600 students have given me lots of experience! If you're a block collector, I hope to give you ideas for putting the blocks together so that you can enjoy using your completed quilt. Perhaps you can use one of the included designs to make that last block you need to finish your quilt.

If you'd like to start a Baltimore-style quilt, this book provides 12 patterns for blocks. They are basic designs, inspired by the antique Baltimore quilts, but with fewer pieces than the originals. Begin by making a few blocks, or plan a small quilt with four designs. Stitch one block each month or work on all the blocks at once. Just do one technique or shape each month. You'll soon be collecting blocks and finishing your quilt.

Come take a place in Baltimore's quilting history with me!

—*Mimi*

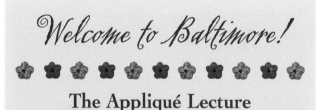

Welcome to Baltimore!

The Appliqué Lecture

When I teach appliqué classes, I like to start with The Appliqué Lecture:

I am going to show you my favorite appliqué techniques. If you've been appliquéing, if you watch appliqué teachers on TV, or if you take other classes, you'll learn that there are many methods for stitching appliqué designs and many different tools to use. All of these techniques are correct. Some methods work better than others in particular situations and with specific fabrics. You can choose different ways to prepare your own appliqué pieces. Your challenge is to try them all, and then decide which ones you like the best!

At first glance, the Baltimore quilts have a special style that gives the impression they all look alike. But take time to really study the quilts and you'll see that each one is unique. You want yours to be special, too!

It helps to research ideas about Baltimore Album quilts before you begin making one. The best way is to gather all your quilting magazines and books, get yourself a cup of tea or coffee, relax in your favorite chair, and just look at pictures for inspiration.

- Search the Internet for photos of quilts. You can find photos on Web sites for museums such as the Maryland Historical Society.

- Go to area quilt shows and take photos of your favorite quilts.

- Make color copies of the photos you like. Keep them in a folder or pin them to your design wall.

- Join an appliqué group, or even start one in your area. You'll get support, ideas, and enthusiasm. The Appliqué Society (TAS) and the Baltimore Appliqué Society have members all over the world. They have wonderful newsletters and Web sites with photos, tips, and ideas. See "Resources" on page 111 for addresses.

- Shop! Take some time to research the fabrics in your local shops and collect the perfect pieces to put in your quilt.

Considering Your Options

Each Baltimore quilt is unique. Here are some things to think about as you do your research.

- Which block designs appeal to you? Do you like wreaths, baskets, vases, or square designs?

- How many blocks do you want? Some quilts have 4 blocks—some have 25! You don't have to decide right now—some stitchers like to just make and collect blocks until they are ready to put together their quilt.

Welcome to Baltimore!

The History of Baltimore Album Quilts

The original Baltimore Album quilts were made in the city of Baltimore, Maryland, in the 1840s and 1850s. These quilts are called "albums" because each block in the quilt is a different and unique design—like the variety of photos in a picture album. There are some pieced blocks, but most of the blocks are appliquéd with gorgeous floral wreaths, baskets, vases, and intricate paper-cut designs. The predominant colors used in the quilts are red and green, with touches of bright blue, brown, gold, and pink. The quilt blocks are made by a variety of quilters and are inked or embroidered with signatures, like autograph albums. Many blocks are also inscribed with favorite sayings and verses. Some of the quilts are "presentation" or friendship quilts, made to honor members of the community. There are quilts with inscriptions to a sea captain as well as to Methodist ministers. Many of the Baltimore quilts have survived in excellent condition. They were probably used only for special occasions.

If you get a chance to see an antique Baltimore Album quilt, you'll be amazed that the stitches are so small, the designs are so beautiful, and the colors are so vivid. It will inspire you to make one for yourself!

- Do you want the blocks set square or on point? If you want them on point, you need to make this decision before you start stitching because it will affect the design orientation on the background fabric.

- When you put your blocks together, do you want them side by side or separated with sashing strips?

- What type of border do you want? An appliquéd border? A vine border or a swag border? Or, do you have the perfect fabric for a basic border?

Oh dear, this sounds like a lot to think about, doesn't it? But after a little enjoyable research, you'll find that you have some preferences. I hope this book will guide you to the answers to some of these questions.

Getting Organized

It feels great to be organized—or at least to look like you are! Here are some ideas to help you get started.

- Clear off a bookshelf where you can keep all your research books and magazines.

- Buy a new plastic container to store your special collection of Baltimore fabrics.

- Use little stickers or masking tape to label your background fabric. You don't want to inadvertently use your block fabric or border fabric for another project and then find out that you don't have enough for your quilt. Make sure you label the binding fabric as well so that you'll have it when you finish your quilt.

- Buy a little photo "brag" book for your collected photos. You can also use the plastic photo pockets to hold 4" square swatches of your fabrics. You'll look and feel organized when you shop for coordinating fabrics for your quilt.

- Use plastic zip-top bags to organize the pieces for each of your blocks.

- Get a clean pizza box to store your finished blocks. It keeps them neat and flat. Decorate the box with quilt photos or fabric!

- Some quilters like to take their quilting books to an office-supply shop or copy center to have the standard binding replaced with a spiral binding. This makes it easy to open the book flat when you're tracing appliqué designs.

Making Decisions

I always tell my students, "It's *your* quilt!" You can use any colors, blocks, or border designs you like. You can rearrange elements in the blocks. Substitute roses for gathered flowers, or buds for gathered blossoms. It's fun, creative, and a great way to express yourself!

There are two basic approaches to making a Baltimore Album quilt:

- Some students know exactly what their quilt will look like. They choose their blocks, decide on a color palette, know what setting they want to use, and make the quilt from start to finish.

- Other students start stitching blocks without making decisions about the entire quilt. They choose some colors and make the first few blocks. As they continue to make blocks, their ideas about the quilt evolve. They find new settings in a magazine, collect new fabrics as they travel, and discover new border ideas.

As you research and work on your blocks, be open to new ideas and give yourself permission to change your plans.

Enlarging or Reducing Patterns

As you do research, I'm sure you'll find designs of different sizes. You can change the size of any design to be consistent with the designs in this book, and it's easy to do if you know a few basic things and have access to a photocopy machine and a calculator. The guy in the copy shop will also help!

The appliqué designs in this book are all based on a 7½" square. They are stitched onto 10½" cut squares of background fabric. When you're considering a new design to add to your quilt, simply measure the size of the pattern design to determine whether it will fit this book's design scale as is or will need to be reduced or enlarged.

If you need to adjust a design's size, divide 7.5 by the measurement of the design. If the resulting number is less than 1.0, you will need to reduce the design to that percentage on a photocopy machine. Conversely, if the resulting number is greater than 1.0, you will need to enlarge the design to that percentage. For example, if you have a 12" design and would like to make it 7½", divide 7.5 by 12. The result is .625, which means (rounding up) that you'll want to reproduce your design at 63% of the original size. If you have a 6" design and would like to make it 7½", divide 7.5 by 6. The result is 1.25, so you'll want to enlarge the design by photocopying it at 125% of the original size. Please note that this formula applies to converting the sizes of *square* blocks, like the ones featured in this book.

Neat Trick!

If you're trying to enlarge a very small photo in a book, photocopy the image, enlarging it several times just until it starts to get blurry. At that point, trace the image and continue enlarging it until it is as big as you want.

Designing Your Quilt

I encourage you to create your own arrangements using your favorite patterns and techniques. There are 12 block designs in this book and they can be used in a variety of quilt settings. Photocopy pages 10 and 15 and use the small blocks to design your quilt. Shade the copies with colored pencils to clarify your options. Cut out the copied blocks and audition them on the provided settings. Use the square blocks for the straight settings on pages 11–14, and the diagonal blocks for the settings on pages 16–18.

Block Ideas: Create balance in the design of your quilt with the block patterns you choose.

- Balance the edges of your quilt by placing four square-shaped designs in the corners of your setting.

- Balance quilts with more than 12 blocks by placing similar block designs directly opposite or diagonally across from each other.

- If you're using four blocks in your quilt, balance designs in opposite diagonal blocks.

- Use one of your favorite block designs in the center of your quilt.

- Start stitching one block at a time and don't worry about the entire quilt until you have made a few blocks.

Fabric Ideas: Another way to create balance in the design of your quilt is with your choice of fabrics.

- Repeat each fabric at least three times in the blocks in the quilt.

- Repeat a flower color or duplicate a flower fabric in a bud.

- If you're using four blocks in your quilt, balance fabrics and colors in opposite diagonal blocks.

- Use a window template to help you select fabrics. See "Look through the Window" on page 20.

- Use a fabric paste-up to audition your fabrics and help you make choices. See "Fabric Paste-ups" on page 20.

Quilt Ideas: After you've made several blocks, begin to think about the whole quilt.

- In addition to using the small blocks on pages 10 and 15, take digital photos of your finished blocks. Print them out and cut them into squares. Use these to make decisions about the layout of your quilt design.

- Pin your blocks to a design wall. Step back and look at your designs.

- Lay the blocks on your bed and take a photo.

- Baltimore quilts are usually square, but a rectangular quilt is another option to consider.

Single Blocks: You may find that you change your mind about including a block or two that you've made. These blocks also make great small wall hangings, pillows, pillow shams, or gifts for friends.

- Sew borders to one block to make a wall hanging.

- Frame a block on point by adding triangles and borders.

Finding Time to Make Your Quilt: I met with a group of ladies who call their group "Baltimore or Bust!" They get together to encourage each other to finish their Baltimore quilts. Here are some of their ideas!

- Join a group—or start one!

- Invite an appliqué buddy to get together to stitch.

- Set small goals for finishing blocks. They call these "Baltimore Baby Steps."

- Schedule your sewing time.

- Prepare a few appliqué pieces to make them portable and ready to sew when you have some time.

- Focus on one shape (leaves) or technique (gathered flowers) at a time.

Think Outside the Block

Appliqué designs translate beautifully to embroidered bluework or redwork. You can even use multiple thread colors.

*"Baltimore Bluework" by Karan Flanscha,
14¼" x 14¼"*

- When you have some blocks finished, lay them out on a table and brainstorm layout ideas with your friends. They will also help you decide which blocks you still need to complete your quilt, or how to quilt your project.

- Go on a retreat with friends or take part in a guild sew-a-thon. Oh—and don't forget to appliqué!

- Don't put your blocks away. Keep them pinned to a flannel board or design wall where you can see them. They will inspire you to keep stitching!

- And, when you just can't sew, you can dream. Get out your quilt books and simply enjoy the beauty of the photos!

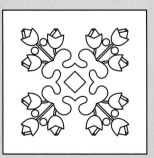  

Blocks for straight settings

Photocopy this page, and then cut out the blocks.
Use them with the settings on pages 11–14 to audition quilt designs.

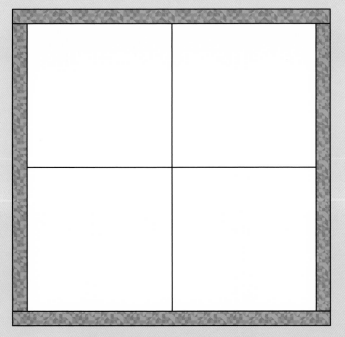

4-block straight setting without sashing.
Use with copied blocks from page 10.

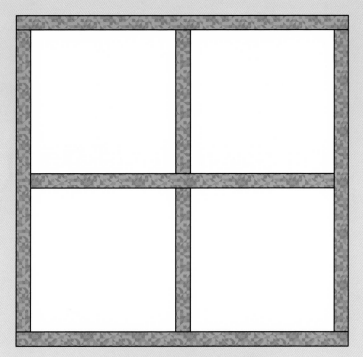

4-block straight setting with sashing.
Use with copied blocks from page 10.

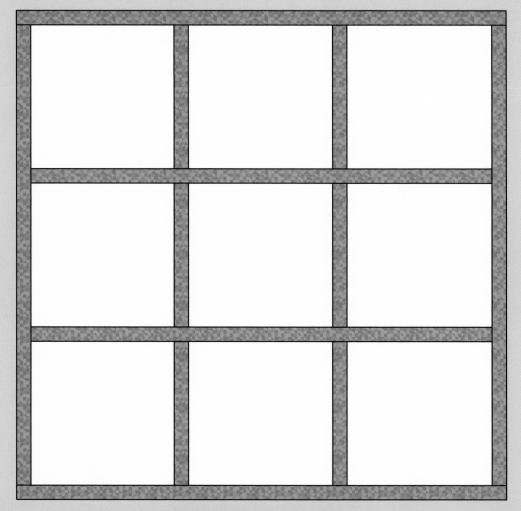

9-block straight setting with sashing.
Use with copied blocks from page 10.

12-block straight setting with sashing.
Use with copied blocks from page 10.

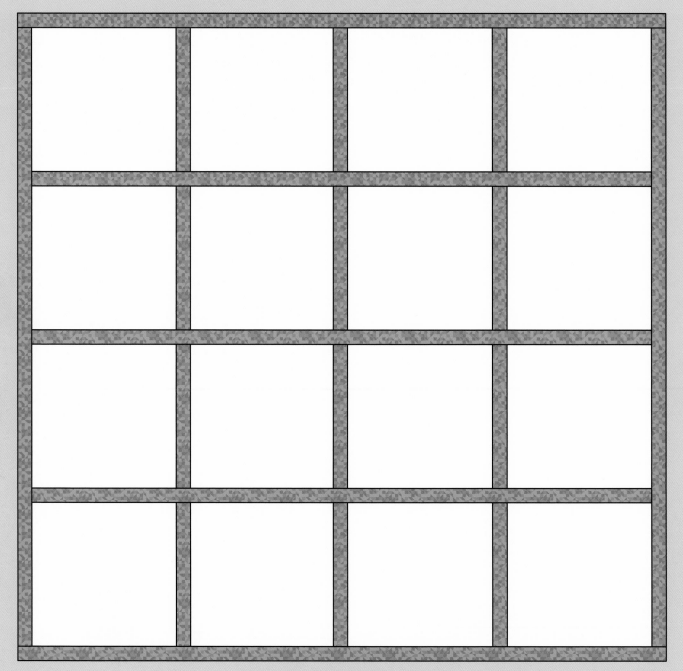

16-block straight setting with sashing.
Use with copied blocks from page 10.

Blocks for diagonal settings
Photocopy this page, and then cut out the blocks.
Use them with the settings on pages 16–18 to audition quilt designs.

15

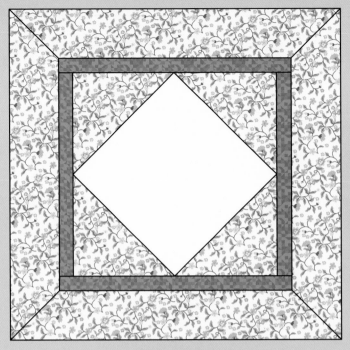

1-block diagonal setting.
Use with copied blocks from page 15.

4-block diagonal setting without sashing.
Use with copied blocks from page 15.

5-block diagonal setting with sashing.
Use with copied blocks from page 15.

13-block diagonal setting with sashing.
Use with copied blocks from page 15.

The best place to shop for appliqué fabrics is at your favorite quilt shop. Take this book with you and you'll find quilters who will help you choose just the right fabrics for your project. Most Baltimore Album quilts are predominantly red and green on a cream background, but this is your quilt—you can make it in any color combination you like!

Fabrics made of 100% cotton are easier to appliqué than synthetic fabrics, which fray more than cotton and are often slippery. Sometimes, however, the perfect fabric contains synthetic fibers, and it's worth a little extra care to use that fabric in your design.

When you choose fabrics for Baltimore-style appliqué projects, you need fabric for three purposes: the background, the appliqué piece, and the backing.

Background Fabrics

Appliqué background fabrics are usually light, solid colors or small prints that complement the appliqué design. Avoid choosing prints or stripes that are too bold; they may compete with the appliquéd design.

White background fabrics add brightness and clarity to your appliqués. Off-white backgrounds enhance the richness of darker appliqué palettes. White-on-white prints are lovely choices for stitchers who prefer a subtle print rather than a solid background. A fabulous tea-dyed print can give an antique glow to quilts. Appliquéing onto a dark background creates a dramatic effect.

If you choose white-on-white background fabrics, be careful to select those with a somewhat open pattern. You might have trouble hand stitching through the white print if the design is too dense. If you are planning to stitch an appliquéd border, remember to purchase enough background fabric for those borders.

Welcome to Baltimore!

The Great Audition

If you already have some of your appliqué fabrics, take some small pieces with you to the store. It may help if you cut the fabrics into leaves or flowers and lay them on a potential background fabric. Walk about 15 feet away, and then turn to look at the pieces. Do you like the way they pair with the background fabric? Can you see them clearly? This auditioning process also works when you're trying to establish contrast between appliqué pieces.

Appliqué Pieces

Traditionally, Baltimore Album quilts are made with a palette of red and green fabrics, plus touches of blue, pink, brown, and yellowish gold. This color scheme is always appropriate, but it's also fun to create the designs in soft pastels, brighter folk-art colors, or shades of a single color, such as blue.

To determine a color palette for your Baltimore-style quilt, do some research and shop for fabrics that make your heart sing! If you find a beautiful multicolored print, this inspiration fabric is the perfect starting point for your fabric collection. Use that print to help you select a variety of fabrics for your color scheme. An inspiration fabric may also make the perfect border for your quilt! Sometimes inspiration fabrics have colored dots along the selvage, and you can use the dots to choose coordinating fabrics for the appliqué pieces. In addition to the proper color, consider the print size (scale) for the pattern you're stitching. In effect, you're painting the designs with fabric.

Solid-colored fabrics are always safe to use, but printed fabrics make designs exciting. They also help conceal stitches along appliqué edges. Fabric printed in multiple values of one color can be very effective when used for flowers and leaves. These tone-on-tone fabrics, such as dark green printed over a lighter green, look like a solid but have subtle texture. In addition, you might find a printed design that could represent veins in leaves or shadows in flower petals.

Tone-on-tone prints add dimension to appliqués.

It's wonderful to use fabrics printed with floral images because you can fussy cut whole flowers or individual petals and leaves to add realism to your appliqués. Refer to "Fussy Cutting" on page 37. Use basket-weave prints for baskets or wood-grain prints for stems. Nature prints often include flowers and leaves. Large-scale prints may seem inappropriate for appliqué, but a small piece cut from a specific area may make the perfect flower petal or bird's wing. If you look at an appliquér's stash of fabric, you often find pieces that look like Swiss cheese!

Be brave and try using the right and wrong sides of the same fabric to shade leaves, flowers, and bows. At first, it might seem strange to use the wrong side, but it often creates a wonderful effect.

Look through the Window

Referring to "Window Template" on page 37, use a paper window template to help you decide which fabric to use. Trace the appliqué piece onto paper and cut it out to create a window. Move the window over your fabric to get a preview of your appliqué piece.

Backing Fabric

You'll also need fabric for the back of your quilt. Use a plain fabric or choose a print that coordinates with your design. A printed fabric will help to hide your quilting stitches on the back. Make sure that the quality of your background fabric is comparable to that used on the front of your quilt. For larger quilts, I like to use extra-wide backing fabrics to avoid a seam on the back of my quilt.

Fabric Paste-ups

How can you be sure you've chosen the right fabrics for your quilt? If you have enough fabric, make a paste-up using your fabrics before you start to stitch. Trace or photocopy your pattern on a sheet of paper, cut the appliqué shapes out of your fabrics, and glue them to the design. Auditioning fabric in this manner helps you make decisions about color arrangements before you begin stitching. You can also trim the paper away around the design and place it on the background fabric to see how it looks on that background. Use the paste-up as a placement guide for the fabrics when you stitch.

Fabric Preparation

Prewash all fabric to preshrink it and to test for colorfastness. Wash dark and light colors separately. Sometimes it is necessary to wash and rinse dark-colored fabrics several times to get rid of excess dye. Many quilters use Retayne (for commercially dyed fabrics), Synthrapol (for hand dyes), or dye magnets such as the ones made by Woolite to prevent the colors from bleeding onto each other when the quilt is laundered. To test a fabric for colorfastness, cut a small piece, wet it, and place it on a scrap of background fabric. If color shows up on the background scrap, wash the fabric again, or choose a different fabric. Take the time to prewash your fabrics.

Before cutting, press fabrics to remove wrinkles. Cutting from perfectly smooth fabric makes it more likely that your pieces will be sized accurately. Some quilters use spray starch or sizing to give the fabrics a little extra body. Other quilters, however, feel that sizing creates drag on the needle as they stitch. Try stitching both sized and unsized fabric to determine your preference.

Determining Yardage and Cutting

Before you buy your fabric and cut your quilt pieces, please read to the end of this book in order to understand the entire process.

Use the following yardage requirements as a general guideline when planning your quilt and purchasing fabrics. Depending on the size of your quilt, purchase fat quarters or ½-yard pieces for your appliqué fabrics.

All of the settings show quilts with basic borders in a floral fabric. If you want an appliquéd border, each setting will indicate the amount of extra background fabric you need to purchase. For appliquéd swag borders, you should buy one extra yard of fabric for the swags. For vine borders, buy at least a ½ yard of extra green fabric.

Exact measurements are given for cutting all sashing strips and borders. Some quilters like to cut borders a few inches longer and then trim them to the exact size of their quilt center. The outer-border measurements already include an extra 2" in length to allow 1" at each end to assist in mitering the corners. Refer to "Borders with Mitered Corners" on page 97 for additional information.

4-Block Straight Setting with or without Sashing

Finished Quilt: 35½" x 35½" with sashing • 34½" x 34½" without sashing • Finished Block: 10"

MATERIALS

All yardages are based on 42"-wide fabric.

⅞ yard of floral print for outer border*

¾ yard of light fabric for block backgrounds

¼ to ½ yard each of assorted prints for appliqué pieces

¼ yard of fabric for inner border

⅛ yard of fabric for sashing

⅓ yard of fabric for binding

1¼ yards of fabric for backing

40" x 40" piece of batting

This yardage is for a quilt with a floral-print border. If you want appliquéd borders, purchase ⅞ yard of light fabric in addition to the fabric for the block backgrounds and cut the border strips 6½" x 37½" from the crosswise grain of the fabric.

CUTTING

For the borders, the first set of cutting measurements is for a quilt with sashing. For a quilt without sashing, use the measurements in parentheses.

From the background fabric, cut:
2 strips, 11½" x 42"; crosscut into 4 squares,
   11½" x 11½"

From the sashing fabric, cut:
2 strips, 1½" x 42"; crosscut into 2 strips,
   1½" x 10½", and 1 strip, 1½" x 21½"

From the inner-border fabric, cut:
2 strips, 1½" x 21½" (20½")
2 strips, 1½" x 23½" (22½")

From the floral print, cut:
4 strips, 6½" x 37½" (36½")

From the binding fabric, cut:
4 strips, 2" x 42"

9-Block Straight Setting with or without Sashing

Finished Quilt: 46½" x 46½" with sashing • 44½" x 44½" without sashing • Finished Block: 10"

MATERIALS

All yardages are based on 42"-wide fabric.

1½ yards of floral print for outer border*

1⅛ yards of light fabric for block backgrounds

¼ to ½ yard each of assorted prints for appliqué pieces

¼ yard of fabric for inner border

¼ yard of fabric for sashing

⅜ yard of accent fabric for binding

2⅞ yards of fabric for backing

51" x 51" piece of batting

This yardage is for a quilt with a floral-print border. If you want appliquéd borders, purchase 1½ yards of light fabric in addition to the fabric for the block backgrounds and cut the border strips 6½" x 48½" from the lengthwise grain of the fabric.

CUTTING

For the borders, the first set of cutting measurements is for a quilt with sashing. For a quilt without sashing, use the measurements in parentheses.

From the background fabric, cut:
3 strips, 11½" x 42"; crosscut into 9 squares, 11½" x 11½"

From the sashing fabric, cut:
6 strips, 1½" x 42"; crosscut into 6 strips, 1½" x 10½", and 2 strips, 1½" x 32½"

From the inner-border fabric, cut:
2 strips, 1½" x 32½" (30½")
2 strips, 1½" x 34½" (32½")

From the floral print, cut:
4 strips, 6½" x 48½" (46½"), from the lengthwise grain

From the binding fabric, cut:
5 strips, 2" x 42"

12-Block Straight Setting with or without Sashing

Finished Quilt: 46½" x 57½" with sashing • 44½" x 54½" without sashing • Finished Block: 10"

MATERIALS

All yardages are based on 42"-wide fabric.

1⅞ yards of floral print for outer border*

1½ yards of light fabric for block backgrounds

1⅛ yards of fabric for inner border

⅓ yard of fabric for sashing

¼ to ½ yard each of assorted prints for appliqué pieces

½ yard of fabric for binding

2⅞ yards of fabric for backing (2 widths pieced horizontally)

51" x 62" piece of batting

*This yardage is for a quilt with a floral-print border. If you want appliquéd borders, purchase 1⅞ yards of light fabric in addition to the fabric for the block backgrounds and cut 2 border strips 6½" x 48½", and 2 border strips 6½" x 59½" from the lengthwise grain of the fabric.

CUTTING

For the borders, the first set of cutting measurements is for a quilt with sashing. For a quilt without sashing, use the measurements in parentheses.

From the background fabric, cut:
4 strips, 11½" x 42"; crosscut into 12 squares, 11½" x 11½"

From the sashing fabric, cut:
6 strips, 1½" x 42"; crosscut into 8 strips, 1½" x 10½", and 3 strips, 1½" x 32½"

From the inner-border fabric, cut:
2 strips, 1½" x 43½" (40½"), from the lengthwise grain

From the remaining width of the fabric, cut:
2 strips, 1½" x 34½" (32½")

From the floral print, cut:
2 strips, 6½" x 48½" (46½"), from the lengthwise grain
2 strips, 6½" x 59½" (56½"), from the lengthwise grain

From the binding fabric, cut:
6 strips, 2" x 42"

16-Block Straight Setting with or without Sashing

Finished Quilt: 57½" x 57½" with sashing • 54½" x 54½" without sashing • Finished Block: 10"

MATERIALS

All yardages are based on 42"-wide fabric.

2⅛ yards of light fabric for block backgrounds

1⅞ yards of floral print for outer border*

1½ yards of fabric for inner border

1½ yards of fabric for sashing

¼ to ½ yard each of assorted prints for appliqué pieces

½ yard of fabric for binding

3½ yards of fabric for backing

62" x 62" piece of batting

This yardage is for a quilt with a floral-print border. If you want appliquéd borders, purchase 1⅞ yards of light fabric in addition to the fabric for the block backgrounds and cut the border strips 6½" x 59½" from the lengthwise grain of the fabric.

CUTTING

For the borders, the first set of cutting measurements is for a quilt with sashing. For a quilt without sashing, use the measurements in parentheses.

From the background fabric, cut:
6 strips, 11½" x 42"; crosscut into 16 squares, 11½" x 11½"

From the sashing fabric, cut:
3 strips, 1½" x 43½", from the lengthwise grain
From the remainder of the fabric, cut:
12 strips, 1½" x 10½"

From the inner-border fabric, cut:
2 strips, 1½" x 43½" (40½"), from the lengthwise grain
2 strips, 1½" x 45½" (42½"), from the lengthwise grain

From the floral print, cut:
4 strips, 6½" x 59½" (56½"), from the lengthwise grain

From the binding fabric, cut:
6 strips, 2" x 42"

1-Block Diagonal Setting

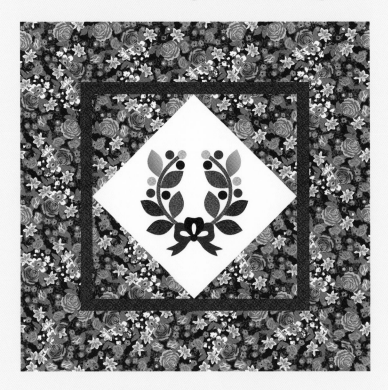

Finished Quilt: 28⅝" x 28⅝" • Finished Block: 10"

MATERIALS

All yardages are based on 42"-wide fabric.

1⅛ yards of floral print for setting triangles and outer border*

½ yard of light fabric for block background

¼ to ½ yard each of assorted prints for appliqué pieces

⅛ yard of fabric for inner border

⅓ yard of fabric for binding

1 yard of fabric for backing

33" x 33" piece of batting

This yardage is for a quilt with a floral-print border. If you want appliquéd borders, purchase ⅞ yard of light fabric in addition to the fabric for the block background and cut the border strips 6½" x 30⅝" from the crosswise grain of the fabric.

CUTTING

From the background fabric, cut:
1 square, 11½" x 11½"

From the floral print, cut:
2 squares, 8" x 8"; cut once diagonally to yield 4 half-square triangles
4 strips, 6½" x 30⅝"

From the inner-border fabric, cut:
2 strips, 1½" x 14¼"
2 strips, 1½" x 16¾"

From the binding fabric, cut:
4 strips, 2" x 42"

4-Block Diagonal Setting

Finished Quilt: 42¾" x 42¾" • Finished Block: 10"

MATERIALS

All yardages are based on 42"-wide fabric.

1⅛ yards of floral print for center block, setting triangles, and outer border*

¾ yard of light fabric for block backgrounds

¼ to ½ yard each of assorted prints for appliqué pieces

¼ yard of fabric for inner border

⅜ yard of fabric for binding

2⅝ yards of fabric for backing

47" x 47" piece of batting

*This yardage is for a quilt with a floral-print border. If you want appliquéd borders, purchase 1⅜ yards of light fabric in addition to the fabric for the block backgrounds and cut the border strips 6½" x 44⅜" from the length-wise grain of the fabric.

CUTTING

From the background fabric, cut:
2 strips, 11½" x 42"; crosscut into 4 squares, 11½" x 11½"

From the floral print, cut:
1 strip, 15⅜" x 42"; crosscut into 1 square, 15⅜" x 15⅜". Cut twice diagonally to yield 4 quarter-square triangles. Use the remainder of the strip to cut 2 squares, 8" x 8"; cut once diagonally to yield 4 half-square triangles.

4 strips, 6½" x 44¾", from the lengthwise grain of the remaining fabric. Use the remaining width of the fabric to cut 1 square, 10½" x 10½".

From the inner-border fabric, cut:
2 strips, 1½" x 28¾"
2 strips, 1½" x 30¾"

From the binding fabric, cut:
5 strips, 2" x 42"

27

5-Block Diagonal Setting with Sashing

Finished Quilt: 45½" x 45½" • Finished Block: 10"

MATERIALS

All yardages are based on 42"-wide fabric.

1⅞ yards of floral print for setting triangles and outer border*

¾ yard of light fabric for block backgrounds

⅓ yard of fabric for sashing

¼ to ½ yard each of assorted prints for appliqué pieces

¼ yard of fabric for inner border

⅜ yard of fabric for binding

2⅞ yards of fabric for backing

50" x 50" piece of batting

This yardage is for a quilt with a floral-print border. If you want appliquéd borders, purchase 1½ yards of light fabric in addition to the fabric for the block backgrounds and cut the border strips 6½" x 47½" from the lengthwise grain of the fabric.

CUTTING

From the background fabric, cut:
2 strips, 11½" x 42"; crosscut into 5 squares, 11½" x 11½"

From the sashing fabric, cut:
6 strips, 1½" x 42"; crosscut into:
8 strips, 1½" x 10½"
2 strips, 1½" x 12½"
2 strips, 1½" x 34½"

From the floral print, cut:
1 square, 15⅜" x 15⅜"; cut twice diagonally to yield 4 quarter-square triangles
4 strips, 6½" x 47½", from the lengthwise grain

From the remaining width of the fabric, cut:
2 squares, 8" x 8"; cut once diagonally to yield 4 half-square triangles

From the inner-border fabric, cut:
2 strips, 1½" x 31½"
2 strips, 1½" x 33½"

From the binding fabric, cut:
5 strips, 2" x 42"

13-Block Diagonal Setting with or without Sashing

Finished Quilt: 61⅛" x 61⅛" with sashing • 56⅞" x 56⅞" without sashing • Finished Block: 10"

MATERIALS

All yardages are based on 42"-wide fabric.

2⅜ yards of floral print for setting triangles and outer border*

1¾ yards of light fabric for block backgrounds

1¾ yards of fabric for sashing

1⅝ yards of fabric for inner border

¼ to ½ yard each of assorted prints for appliqué pieces

½ yard of fabric for binding

3¾ yards of fabric for backing

65" x 65" piece of batting

This yardage is for a quilt with a floral-print border. If you want appliquéd borders, purchase 2 yards of light fabric in addition to the fabric for the block backgrounds and cut the border strips 6½" x 63⅛" from the lengthwise grain of the fabric.

CUTTING

For the borders, the first set of cutting measurements is for a quilt with sashing. For a quilt without sashing, use the measurements in parentheses.

From the background fabric, cut:
5 strips, 11½" x 42"; crosscut into 13 squares, 11½" x 11½"

From the sashing fabric, cut:
2 strips, 1½" x 56½", from the lengthwise grain

From the remaining width of the fabric, cut:
18 strips, 1½" x 10½"
2 strips, 1½" x 12½"
2 strips, 1½" x 34½"

From the floral print, cut:
2 squares, 15⅜" x 15⅜"; cut twice diagonally to yield 8 quarter-square triangles
4 strips, 6½" x 63⅛" (58⅞"), from the lengthwise grain

From the remaining width of the fabric, cut:
2 squares, 8" x 8"; cut once diagonally to yield 4 half-square triangles

From the inner-border fabric, cut:
2 strips, 1½" x 47⅛" (42⅞"), from the lengthwise grain
2 strips, 1½" x 49⅛" (44⅞"), from the lengthwise grain

From the binding fabric, cut:
7 strips, 2" x 42"

These are some of the many products available in quilt and fabric shops that will help you successfully complete your appliqué projects.

Bias bars: These flat, narrow metal bars are available in a variety of widths. They are helpful when making stems for your appliqué design; they should be used with bias-cut fabric strips.

Fabric markers: Choose from a variety of fabric markers to transfer appliqué designs onto background fabric and to trace appliqué pieces. Use silver marking pencils, water-erasable pens, or fine-lead mechanical pencils for light fabrics. For dark fabrics, use sharp chalk pencils in white or yellow. It is always wise to test the markers on a scrap of fabric to make sure the marks can be removed easily.

Freezer paper: Freezer paper is available at most grocery stores and quilt shops. The shiny, plastic-coated side of the paper softens and sticks to fabric when you apply a dry, warm iron to the uncoated side. Use freezer paper to make templates for freezer-paper appliqué techniques.

Glue stick: A water-soluble glue stick is handy for glue basting seam allowances as well as basting appliqué pieces to background fabric.

Iron: Use a steam iron to press your fabric before you appliqué and to press finished blocks. Use a dry iron to attach freezer-paper templates to your fabric.

Needle threader: If a needle is difficult to thread, use a needle threader to insert the thread through the eye of the needle.

Needles: When you choose a needle for hand appliqué, size is very important. A sharp, fine needle glides easily through the edge of appliqué pieces, creating small, invisible stitches. In needle sizes, the higher the number, the finer the needle. Use sizes 10 to 12 for best results.

Some appliqué stitchers use short quilting needles called Betweens because they feel that short needles give them greater control. Official appliqué needles are longer and are called Sharps. An even longer needle, called a straw needle or milliner's needle, works well for needle turning the appliqué edge as you stitch it to the background. Try different needles to find the one most comfortable for you. My favorite is a #10 straw needle.

Between	⸻
Sharp	⸻
Milliner's	⸻

Permanent marker: Use a fine-tipped permanent marker to trace designs onto template plastic and to write on your fabric.

Pins: Small ½" or ¾" straight pins are wonderful for pin basting because they aren't as likely as longer pins to catch the thread as you stitch.

Plastic multicircle stencil: Found in most office and art-supply stores, this handy stencil makes it easy to draw perfectly round shapes. This is the best tool for making circles!

Plastic zip-top bags: What did we do before zip-top bags were invented? They keep your appliqué pieces organized and clean.

Rotary-cutting equipment: A rotary cutter, mat, and ruler will help you cut your blocks, borders, sashing, and binding. My favorite rulers are 4" x 18" for cutting strips and 10½" square for trimming completed blocks.

Scissors: Small scissors with sharp blades that cut all the way to the point are often a stitcher's prized possession. You'll also need scissors to cut paper or plastic templates.

Sewing light: A true-color light, such as an Ott-Lite, or a magnifying light will help you see your appliqué more easily as you stitch. If you're right-handed, the light should shine over your left shoulder; if you're left-handed, it should shine over your right shoulder.

Sewing machine: Make sure your sewing machine is in good working order with a new needle when you sew your quilt blocks together. I love a ¼" presser foot that helps to keep the seam allowances accurate.

Tape: Use Scotch Removable Magic Tape to anchor your fabric to your pattern while you transfer the design onto your background fabric. Unlike other tapes, this one won't rip the paper or fray your fabric.

Template plastic: Use template plastic to make patterns for appliqué pieces. Cardboard templates are an option, but heat-resistant plastic templates are more durable and accurate, and even withstand ironing.

Thimble: Use a thimble to protect your finger as you push the needle through your fabric during hand appliqué.

Thread: Appliqué thread should match the color of the appliqué fabric rather than the background fabric. Appliqué designs with many different-colored pieces require many shades of thread. If it isn't possible to match the color exactly, choose thread that is a little darker than the fabric. For appliqué fabrics that are printed with many colors, choose a thread that blends with the predominant color. Sometimes a neutral brown or gray blends perfectly.

I believe that the best thread for stitching appliqués is 100% cotton. It is pliable and blends invisibly into the edges of the appliqués. Size 50 is all-purpose sewing thread and can be found in most sewing stores. Size 60 is a finer thread, which helps make your stitches invisible. If you can't find cotton thread in just the right color, use cotton-covered polyester thread. Some hand stitchers also love to use thin silk thread. Experiment and see which thread you like best.

Always use white or light-colored thread for basting. Dye from dark thread can leave small dots of color on light fabrics when the thread is removed.

Tweezers: A small pair of tweezers makes it easy to remove freezer paper after you've appliquéd a piece to the background.

Your favorite chair and lamp: When you hand appliqué, you'll be more comfortable and have the patience to make smaller stitches if you sit in your favorite chair with a lamp aimed at your work. A cup of tea or coffee also helps!

Welcome to Baltimore!

Appliqué Pillow

One of my favorite appliqué tools is a small pillow. I place it in my lap when I stitch. It makes it easy to see my work, rests my hands and shoulders, improves posture, and is a great pincushion.

1. Use a piece of 8½" x 11" notebook paper as a pattern.

2. Cut out two rectangles, one from white fabric and one from printed fabric, adding ¼" seam allowances to all sides.

3. Sew the rectangles right sides together, using a ¼" seam allowance and leaving a 3" opening on one long side to turn the pillow. Use purchased cording (or make your own) around the pillow edge to make the pillow sturdier.

4. Turn the pillow right side out and stuff firmly with polyester stuffing.

5. Stitch the opening closed by hand and enjoy using your pillow!

Before you appliqué, you need to cut the background blocks, mark the appliqué placement lines, and make templates for the required appliqué pieces. Working carefully and accurately will ensure that your quilt looks great!

Cutting Background Fabric

The Baltimore Basics patterns in this book are all printed full size. The finished size of each block is 10" square. Normally the background fabric would be cut 10½" x 10½" square to include ¼"-wide seam allowances on all sides. However, because appliqué blocks sometimes fray or distort during stitching, I like to cut the squares 1" larger (11½" x 11½") and trim them to the correct size (10½" x 10½") after I've completed the appliqué. If you're left-handed, please reverse the directions listed in the steps that follow.

❶ Place a square ruler on the fabric and cut the first two sides of the square.

❷ Turn the fabric around and line up the newly cut edges with the appropriate measurement on the ruler. Keep the 1" marks on the ruler in the upper-right corner to help you measure. Cut the remaining two sides of the square.

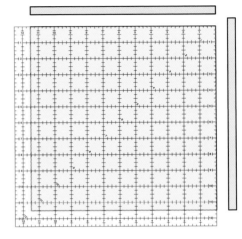

❸ Write your initials in the lower-right corner of each block with a pencil. This serves several purposes. If you're working with a group of other quilters, it will identify which block is yours. It will remind you how to orient the block if your fabric has a one-way floral or striped design. It will indicate the right side of the fabric (yes, there are some stitchers who have appliquéd on the wrong side of the fabric by mistake). And, if you're concerned about the lengthwise or crosswise grain of the fabric, it will help you keep the grain consistent in all of your blocks.

Marking Appliqué Placement Lines

To accurately position the appliqué pieces on the background fabric, mark the design directly onto the fabric.

TRACING ONTO LIGHT BACKGROUNDS

❶ If you're planning a quilt with a straight setting, fold your square of background fabric into quarters. Press the folds at the edges, but gently finger-press in the center of the block.

Place the background fabric right side up over the appliqué pattern. (If you're using a solid background fabric, you can use either side.) Place the folds on the vertical and horizontal lines marked on each pattern, matching the center of the design. Tape your fabric over the pattern using removable tape.

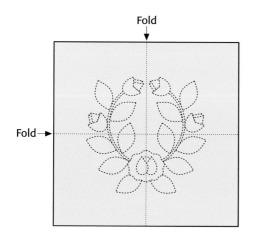

Fold

Fold

If you're planning a quilt with the blocks on point, fold the fabric in quarters diagonally for tracing any of the wreaths, baskets, and vases. Any of the square designs should still be traced as straight-set blocks.

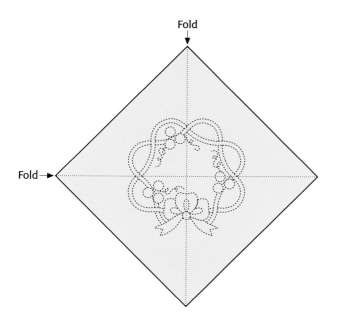

Fold

Fold

2 Trace the design exactly on the lines with a washable pencil or fabric marker. If you aren't certain that the traced lines will wash out, trace slightly inside the pattern lines. The lines will then be covered by the appliquéd pieces after they are stitched, so you don't have to worry about removing the lines. Trace the design using solid or dotted lines.

TRACING ONTO DARK BACKGROUNDS

1 A light box is very helpful when tracing a design onto dark fabric. If you don't have a light box, tape the pattern to a window or glass door on a sunny day. Center your fabric over the pattern and tape the fabric to the glass.

2 Trace the design with a white or yellow chalk pencil.

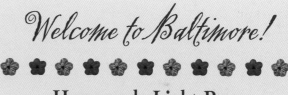

Homemade Light Box

You can create your own light box by opening the leaves of your dining-room table and placing a storm window or sheet of Plexiglas over the opening. Position a lamp or flashlight on the floor below the opening. Place your pattern on the glass and your fabric on top of the pattern. The light will shine through like a light box so that you can easily trace your design.

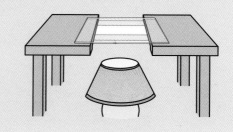

Making Pattern Overlays

If you find it difficult to trace the design onto your background fabric or if you don't wish to mark directly on your background fabric, try a pattern overlay. Some quilters prefer to use this technique when a pattern has many layers of appliqué pieces.

1 Make a pattern overlay by using a permanent marker to trace the pattern onto a piece of clear template plastic that is the same size as your background fabric. You can also use lightweight interfacing, tracing paper, or acetate. Quilters who love this method often recommend Pattern Ease, available in sewing shops.

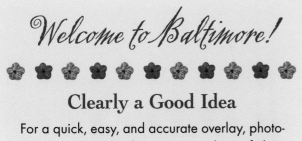

Welcome to Baltimore!

Clearly a Good Idea

For a quick, easy, and accurate overlay, photocopy or scan your design onto a sheet of clear acetate. This product is generally available in office-supply stores or copy centers.

2 Place the pattern overlay on the background fabric. To position each appliqué piece, lift up the pattern overlay, slide the piece under the appropriate marking, and then pin or baste the appliqué to the background fabric.

Slide appliqué shapes under the overlay
to place them on the background.

Making Templates and Cutting Appliqué Pieces

Trace the pieces of each appliqué design directly from the pattern onto plastic or freezer paper to create the templates you need. Prepare your templates accurately to ensure the best results.

MAKING AND USING PLASTIC TEMPLATES

Templates made from template plastic are durable and can be used for most appliqué techniques.

1 Place the plastic over the pattern and trace each design piece with a fine-tipped permanent marker. Don't add seam allowances. If a design motif is repeated in a quilt, you only need one plastic template for each motif.

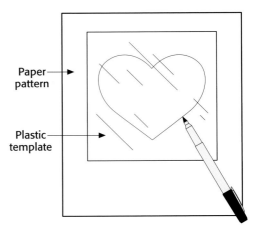

Paper
pattern

Plastic
template

2 Cut out the templates on the traced lines so that they are the exact size of the original pieces.

3 Label the front of each template with the pattern name and template number. This indicates the right side of the template.

Curved basket
6

To use your plastic templates:

1 Place the plastic template right side up on the right side of the appliqué fabric. Refer to "Placing Templates on the Fabric" on page

37. Place a sheet of fine sandpaper under your fabric to prevent it from slipping as you work. A small piece of double-sided tape on the back of the template will help to keep the template in place as well.

2 Trace around the template, marking on the right side of the fabric. Use a pencil or a marker that is appropriate for your fabric. When you trace pieces onto your fabric, leave at least ½" separation between pieces.

3 Cut out each fabric piece, adding an approximate ¼"-wide seam allowance to all sides. The seam allowance will be turned under to create the finished edge of the appliqué.

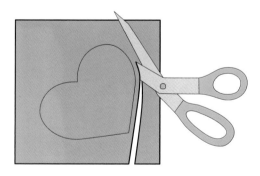

MAKING AND USING FREEZER-PAPER TEMPLATES

Use freezer-paper templates for all freezer-paper appliqué techniques. For repeated designs, make a plastic template and trace around it the required number of times onto the freezer paper. This helps ensure that all pieces of one shape are the same size.

1 Place the freezer paper, coated side down, over the pattern, and trace each design onto the paper side with a fine-lead mechanical pencil.

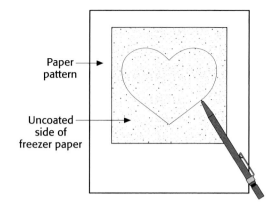

2 Cut out the templates on the traced lines so that they are the exact size of the original pattern pieces.

3 Here's a suggestion for cutting multiple freezer-paper templates of the same shape. First, cut up to four layers of freezer paper roughly the same size as your pattern piece. Trace the design onto the top layer and then staple the layers together by placing a few staples in the space that will be cut away. The staples will hold the layers together as you cut, ensuring accurate templates.

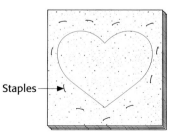

Freezer-paper templates can be used either on the top or on the back of the appliqué fabric.

Using freezer paper on the top:

1. For this method, trace all shapes onto freezer paper as they appear on the pattern. Don't trace asymmetrical designs in reverse.

2. Place the freezer-paper template with the coated side against the right side of the appliqué fabric. Leave at least ½" between pieces. Refer to "Placing Templates on the Fabric" on page 37.

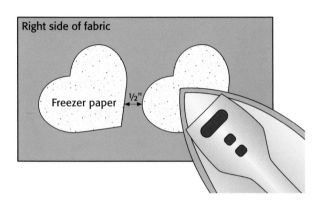

3. Press the freezer paper using a hot, dry iron. Let the piece cool.

4. Cut out the fabric appliqué pieces, adding an approximate ¼"-wide seam allowance around the outside edge of each shape. To ensure that the freezer paper stays in place, you may wish to baste along the edge of the paper. This is especially helpful with large pieces.

Welcome to Baltimore!

Reusable, Stickable Appliqué Templates

You can also cut your appliqué shapes from removable self-stick labels—they adhere well and can be reused several times.

Using freezer paper on the back:

1. For this method, asymmetrical shapes must be traced in reverse. See "Reverse Images" below.

2. Place the freezer-paper template with the coated side against the wrong side of the appliqué fabric. Leave at least ½" between pieces.

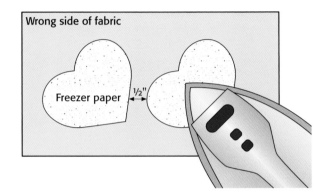

3. Press the freezer paper using a hot, dry iron. Let the piece cool.

4. Cut out the fabric appliqué pieces, adding a generous ¼"-wide seam allowance around the outside edge of each shape.

Welcome to Baltimore!

Reverse Images

Trace symmetrical designs directly from the pattern to the paper. For asymmetrical designs, such as the bird on page 81, you must trace a reverse (mirror) image of the pattern piece. To trace a reverse image, turn the pattern over and place it on a light box or against a bright window, and then trace the pattern onto the freezer paper.

PLACING TEMPLATES ON THE FABRIC

You will create beautiful appliqués if you carefully consider where to cut your fabric. The following information will help you choose the perfect section of your fabric for each appliqué shape.

Grain lines: Appliqué designs don't usually provide grain lines to aid in positioning the templates on the fabric. If possible, place the templates on the appliqué fabric so that the straight grain runs in the same direction as the background fabric.

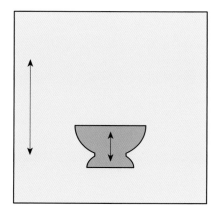

Bias: Designs that have inside points (such as hearts) or curves (such as leaves) should be placed on the bias of the fabric. This diagonal placement prevents fraying at inside points and helps ease fabric around curves.

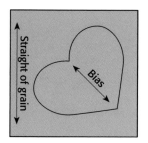

Fussy cutting: For some designs, you can cut an appliqué piece to include a specific part of a printed fabric. Quilters love to fussy cut leaves or flowers that have been printed on the fabric. In this case, disregard grain lines to enjoy the way that the fabric and the appliqué design can work together. Use a window template as described below to help you make decisions.

Window template: To get a special effect from a fabric, trace the appliqué piece onto paper and cut it out to create a window template. Move the window over your fabric to determine the perfect placement for your template before you cut out the appliqué piece.

There are many techniques for preparing the raw edges of appliqué fabric pieces before sewing them to the background fabric. These methods are all correct and successful, although some methods work better than others in particular situations and with specific fabrics. You can choose different ways to prepare your own appliqué pieces. You'll probably like one better than others, but try them all and choose your favorite. Remember The Appliqué Lecture on page 5!

Method One: Traditional Appliqué Preparation

When I first learned to appliqué, this is the method I used. You don't need any special tools, just templates, fabric, needle, and thread.

1. Cut out the appliqué shapes, referring to "Making and Using Plastic Templates" on page 34.

2. Turn under the seam allowances by rolling the seam under a short segment at a time. Turn the traced line to the back of the appliqué piece so that it doesn't show on the front of the appliqué. Clip any inside points if necessary.

3. Hand baste the seam allowance in place, using light-colored thread in your needle. Refer to "Hand-Basting Primer" on page 41.

4. Instead of basting, you can also apply glue stick to the ¼"-wide seam allowance on the wrong side of the appliqué. Wait a few seconds for the glue to get tacky, and then carefully fold the seam allowance to the back of the appliqué piece.

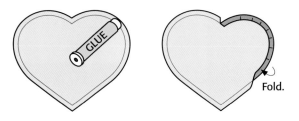

Fold.

5. Use the marked placement lines to pin or baste the prepared appliqué pieces to the background fabric. Refer to "Traditional Appliqué Stitch" on page 47 to stitch the appliqué in place.

6. Remove any basting stitches if necessary.

Method Two: Freezer Paper on Back—Basted Preparation

This is my favorite method! Freezer paper sticks to the fabric and controls the appliqué shape. I like to use this method when I want accuracy in repeated designs.

1. Cut out the appliqué shapes, referring to "Using freezer paper on the back" on page 36.

2. Turn the ¼" seam allowance toward the freezer paper and either baste by hand, referring to "Hand-Basting Primer" on page 41, or use a glue stick to lightly baste it to the paper. Clip any inside points to within a few threads of the freezer paper and fold any outside points.

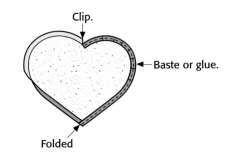

Clip.

Baste or glue.

Folded

3 Use the marked placement lines to pin or baste the prepared appliqué pieces to the background fabric. Refer to "Traditional Appliqué Stitch" on page 47 to stitch the appliqué in place.

4 Remove any basting stitches. Cut a small slit in the background fabric behind the appliqué and remove the freezer paper with tweezers.

Wrong side of background

5 If you've basted with a glue stick, soak the piece in warm water for a few minutes to soften the glue and release the paper. Pull out the paper. After the appliqué dries, press it from the wrong side.

Method Three: Needle-Turn Appliqué Preparation

This preparation method saves time because you don't baste the seam allowances. Use your needle to control the fabric, and be careful not to pull the thread too tightly.

1 Cut out the appliqué shapes, referring to "Making and Using Plastic Templates" on page 34. Add a skimpy ¼" seam allowance when cutting out the shapes.

2 Place the appliqué pieces on the background fabric using the marked placement lines. Pin or baste them securely in place. Position the appliqué as accurately as possible, because the seam allowances will overlap the background markings.

3 Appliqué the shapes in place, referring to "Needle-Turn Appliqué" on page 49.

Needle-Turn Preparation Using Freezer Paper

This technique uses freezer paper for accurate shaping, but eliminates the basting step.

NEEDLE-TURN WITH FREEZER PAPER ON BACK

1 Cut out the appliqué shapes, referring to "Using freezer paper on the back" on page 36. Add a generous seam allowance when you cut out the shapes. Clip any inside points, but don't turn under and baste the seam allowances to the wrong side.

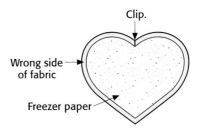

Clip.

Wrong side of fabric

Freezer paper

2 Place the appliqué pieces on the background fabric using the marked placement lines, and position the appliqué as accurately as possible, because the seam allowances will overlap the background markings. Pin or baste them securely in place.

3 Appliqué the shapes in place, referring to "Needle-Turn Appliqué" on page 49. The stiffness of the freezer paper makes it easy to turn under the seam allowances and gives you a smooth edge to work against. The result is a perfectly shaped finished appliqué.

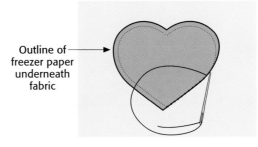

Outline of freezer paper underneath fabric

④ After stitching the appliqués in place, cut a small slit in the background fabric behind the appliqué and remove the freezer paper with tweezers.

NEEDLE-TURN WITH FREEZER PAPER ON TOP

If you don't like the idea of cutting the back of your work to remove the freezer paper after you appliqué, try ironing the freezer paper to the right side of your appliqué fabric.

① Cut out the appliqué shapes, referring to "Using freezer paper on the top" on page 36.

② Securely pin or baste the appliqué pieces to the background fabric using the marked placement lines.

③ Following the shape of the paper, use the tip of your needle to gently turn under the seam allowance, referring to "Needle-Turn Appliqué" on page 49. Turn under the seam allowance at the edge of the freezer paper so that a tiny bit of the fold shows just beyond the edge of the paper. Use the tip of the needle to smooth the fabric along the edge. Then, stitch the appliqué to the background fabric.

④ Peel away the freezer paper when you're finished.

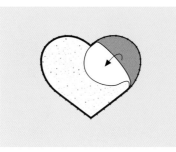

Method Four: Stitch-Marked Appliqué Preparation

This method provides perfect placement for appliqué pieces. It's especially nice for symmetrical designs like the pineapples used in the "Pineapples" block on page 68. Try it!

① Trace the appliqué design on the *wrong* side of the background fabric with a sharp pencil. Refer to "Reverse Images" on page 36 to trace asymmetrical shapes in reverse.

Wrong side of background fabric

② Cut a piece of appliqué fabric slightly larger than the desired shape. Place the background fabric against a light source and place the appliqué fabric over the marked design. The wrong side of the appliqué fabric should be next to the right side of the background fabric. Pin the appliqué fabric in place.

③ Turn the background fabric to the wrong side and sew running stitches along the pencil line, stitching through both layers of fabric. Use a large needle and heavy thread, such as quilting thread, to make perforations in the fabrics. Begin and end with a single knot.

4 On the right side of the appliqué fabric, trim around the appliqué design, adding a skimpy ¼" seam allowance around the edges.

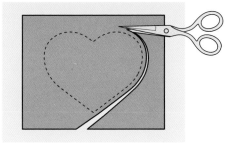

5 Use your small, sharp scissors to clip every third stitch for about 2".

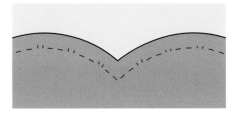

6 Pick out the clipped threads in the first clipped section, needle turn the seam allowance, and appliqué, referring to "Needle-Turn Appliqué" on page 49. The perforations from the basting stitches will help to turn the edges of the appliqué fabric and match the placement line on the background.

7 Continue clipping the threads in sections, remove the clipped threads, and stitch the appliqué to complete the design.

Hand-Basting Primer

Basting is commonly used to prepare the edges of appliqué shapes as well as to secure them to the background fabric prior to stitching. To begin, here are my favorite tips for hand basting the seam allowances of appliqué shapes. Practice basting the edges of a heart-shaped appliqué and you'll feel confident stitching straight edges, curves, and points.

1 Make a freezer paper template and cut an appliqué piece of the heart shape on page 42, referring to "Using freezer paper on the back" on page 36.

2 Thread a needle with an 18" length of light-colored thread. Don't make a knot in the end, because you'll want to easily remove the basting thread later. Instead of starting with a knot, leave a little tail of thread when you start. The paper will hold the thread in place.

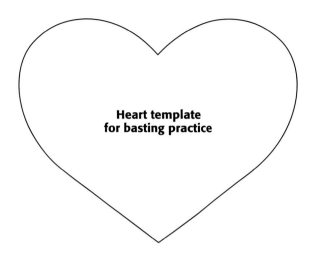

Heart template
for basting practice

Place your freezer-paper template on the bias of the fabric to prevent fraying at the inside points and to help ease the fabric around curves.

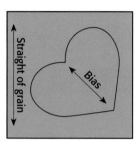

Straight Edges

1 Begin at the point and turn under the straight edge of the heart. Hand baste the heart along the straight edge, folding the seam allowance snugly over and against the freezer-paper heart. Sew through the two layers of fabric and the freezer paper.

2 Look at the right side of the piece while you turn under the fabric and baste. Check that you're maintaining a smooth edge. If you keep your stitches near the fold, you'll be sure to catch the seam allowance underneath.

3 Stop about halfway up one side of the heart.

Outside Curves

1 Baste outside curves by making small running stitches in the seam allowance only. Don't baste through the paper and the right side of the fabric. Gently pull the thread to gather the fabric and ease the seam allowance around the curve for a smooth fit.

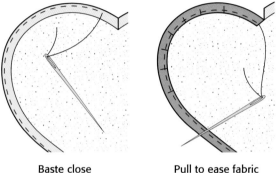

Baste close
to fabric edge.

Pull to ease fabric
around curve.

2 Don't clip the outside curve because clipping creates little bumps along the edge of the appliqué.

3 If little points appear along the curve, you can control them with the tip of your needle when you sew the appliqué to the background.

Inside Points

1 As you finish basting the first curve of your heart, you'll come to the inside point, also known by the term *cleavage*. Carefully clip the seam allowance straight into the cleavage to allow the fabric to turn under easily. Stop clipping about four or five threads from the freezer paper. Don't clip all the way into the point.

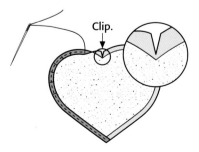

Clip.

2 Use a pencil to mark two Xs on the back of your freezer-paper heart as shown.

3 As you baste the inside point, try this "wonder stitch" to prevent fraying at the clipped point and keep the basting thread away from the inside point while you appliqué. Take a stitch from the clipped edge into the closest X on the back of the heart through to the right side of the fabric. This will gently pull the seam allowance away from the inside point.

Bring the needle back up through the other X. This keeps the thread away from your appliqué stitches at the inside point.

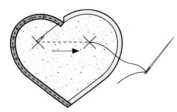

Pull the seam allowance of the second curve snugly over the freezer paper. Insert the needle into the seam allowance and begin basting the second curve, gathering the fullness of the curve.

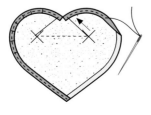

This stitch should "lift and separate" the seam allowance and enhance the cleavage.

4 If there are threads fraying at the inside point, don't force them to turn under. You can sweep them with the tip of the needle when you appliqué. Refer to the "Inside Points" section on page 51 of "Elements of Baltimore-Style Appliqué."

Outside Points

1 As you get to the outside point of the heart, finger-press the remaining seam allowance under. Turn the end over the beginning to form a clean point and baste in place. A small tab of fabric may show on the edge, but you can tuck it under with your needle when you appliqué. This method works great when you can begin and end at the same point.

Fold.

2 There is another good method for preparing outside points. Begin by turning the point of the fabric in toward the appliqué. Apply a small dab of glue stick to hold this in place. Fold the right side under, then the left, to form a sharp point. This technique also works well on leaves.

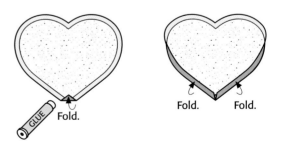

Fold.   Fold.   Fold.

The seam allowances may overlap slightly at the point. They will overlap more on a very sharp point. If the fabric at the point where the seam allowances cross is too thick to baste, push the extra fabric under the point with your needle later when you sew. Baste close to the edge.

Welcome to Baltimore!

Folding the Point

When you fold the point, don't fold it tight against the appliqué shape. Relax a little! Keep the fold 1/16" away from the appliqué, and then the side folds will have room to form a sharp point. This method works well for the points of leaves.

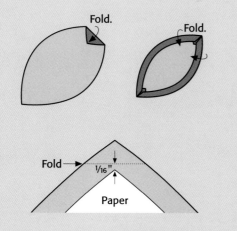

One Last Thing

When you finish basting your appliqué shape, don't tie a knot. Leave a thread tail so that you'll be able to remove your basting threads easily.

Inside Curves

The only basic shape not included in the heart is an inside curve. An inside curve should be clipped in several places (every ¼") so that the seam allowance will relax and turn under smoothly. Clip only halfway through the seam allowance to avoid fraying at the edge of the appliqué. Fold the clipped seam allowance over the edge of the freezer paper and baste.

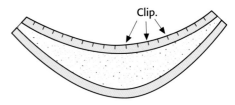

Basting Appliqués to the Background

Now that your appliqué shapes are cut and the seam allowances are basted, you're ready to baste the shapes to the background fabric. This will hold them in place while you appliqué.

Welcome to Baltimore!

One at a Time

When appliquéing, I like to baste and then appliqué one piece in place before adding the next piece—instead of basting all the pieces in place and then proceeding with the appliqué. If I work with too many pieces at once, the appliqué thread gets caught on the other pieces as I stitch.

PIN BASTING

Use several pins to attach the appliqué pieces to the background so that they won't slip out of place. Small ½" to ¾" straight pins—sometimes called sequin or appliqué pins—are wonderful because they tend to not catch on your appliqué thread as you stitch. If you *do* have trouble with threads tangling around the pins as you sew, pin the appliqués in place from the wrong side of the background fabric.

GLUE BASTING

Baste the pieces in place using a water-soluble glue stick. Lightly apply glue stick to the background fabric, keeping glue toward the center of the piece. Don't apply glue along the outer edges where you'll stitch because the glue will stiffen the fabric and make it difficult to sew the appliqué to the background.

After applying the glue, position the appliqué and wait for the glue to dry before sewing. When you're finished, soak the appliqué in warm water to remove the glue.

HAND BASTING

Basting by hand is another option. Use light-colored thread to baste near the edges of the appliqués.

You've cut out your appliqué pieces, prepared the seam allowances, and basted the pieces to the background fabric. It's time to appliqué! But before you stitch your appliqués to the background fabric, take a few minutes to learn some important information about thread.

- Color is very important. If you match the thread color to your appliqué fabric, it will blend in and your stitches will seem smaller and almost invisible. If you can't find the perfect color match, use thread that is a little darker. It will blend into the appliqué fabric, whereas a lighter shade of thread may sparkle and show along the edge.

- Cut a single strand of thread about 18" long. If your thread is too long, it will tangle and you'll have unwanted knots.

- Use a new thread for each appliqué piece. It's tempting to use every inch of your thread, but it frays and loses strength with repeated stitching.

- Thread is smoother in one direction because it is twisted when it is manufactured. You can take advantage of this by cutting and knotting your thread so that it will slide smoothly through the fabric. Refer to "Threading the Needle" below.

Threading the Needle

If you're right-handed, thread the needle before you cut the thread off the spool. Then cut the thread near the spool and tie a knot in the end that you cut.

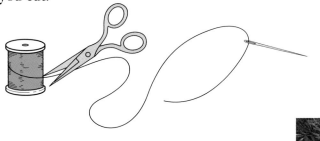

If you're left-handed, tie a knot in the end of the thread while it is still on the spool. Then, measure off 18". Cut the thread near the spool and thread the cut end into the needle. No more twisted threads while you stitch!

- If you have trouble threading the needle, trim the end of the thread at an angle with sharp scissors.

- Try putting the needle onto the thread instead of the thread through the needle. Surprise!

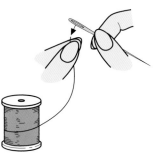

Move the needle toward the thread.

Tying a Quilter's Knot

1. Hold the needle in your sewing hand and the end of the thread in your other hand.

2. Cross the tail of thread in front of the needle, and hold the thread securely between your forefinger and thumb.

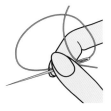

Hold thread between thumb and forefinger.

3 Move the thread away from you, wrapping the thread around the needle three times.

Wrap thread around
needle three times.

4 Hold the wrapped thread between your finger and thumb and gently pull the needle through the wraps.

Pull needle through wraps.

5 A neat knot will appear at the end of your thread.

Traditional Appliqué Stitch

The traditional appliqué stitch is appropriate for sewing all areas of your appliqué designs. It works well on straight areas as well as on sharp points and curves.

1 Thread your needle with a single strand of thread approximately 18" long. Tie a knot in one end. To hide your knot as you begin, slip your needle into the seam allowance from the wrong side of the appliqué piece (but not through the background fabric), bringing it out through the fold line. The knot will be hidden inside the seam allowance and your work will look very tidy.

2 Stitch along the outer edge of the appliqué. If you're right-handed, stitch from right to left. If you're left-handed, stitch from left to right. Start the first stitch by bringing your needle straight out of the appliqué and inserting it into the background fabric directly opposite the point where the thread exited the appliqué.

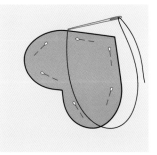

3 Move the needle forward about ⅛" under the background fabric to take a stitch parallel to the edge of the appliqué. Then bring it through to the right side of the background fabric, just at the edge of the appliqué. As you continue, pierce the edge of the appliqué piece, catching only one or two threads of the folded edge.

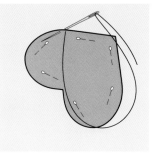

4 Bring the needle straight off the appliqué edge and back into the background fabric. Let your needle travel forward another ⅛" under the background, bringing it up again to barely catch the edge of the appliqué.

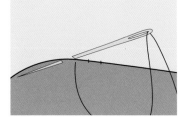

Give the thread a slight tug and continue stitching. The only visible parts of the stitch are small dots of thread along the appliqué edge.

The part of the stitch that travels forward will be seen as a ⅛"-long stitch on the wrong side of the background fabric.

Wrong side of fabric

Stitch Support

Support your fabric by holding the index finger or middle finger of your nonsewing hand directly under the appliqué. As you stitch, push the needle underneath until it gently touches your finger. Then, move the needle back up through the fabric.

Stitching Tips

- As you sew, keep your needle parallel to the appliqué edge with each forward stitch.
- Give the thread a slight tug so that it blends into the appliqué.
- Keep the length of your stitches consistent as you stitch along the straight edges. Make smaller stitches when you get to curves and points.
- And finally—stop stitching while you still have enough thread to tie a final knot!

5 When you get to the end of your appliqué stitching, or you're nearly out of thread, pull your needle through to the wrong side. Behind the appliqué piece, take two small stitches, making a simple knot by bringing your needle through the stitch loops.

6 Before you cut your thread, take a moment to make the back of your work as neat as the front. Take one more small stitch behind the appliqué to direct the tail of the thread under the appliqué fabric. Clip the thread so that it won't show.

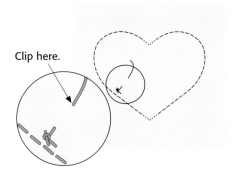

Clip here.

Needle-Turn Appliqué

Prepare the appliqué pieces using "Method Three: Needle-Turn Appliqué Preparation" on page 39. Use the traditional appliqué stitch to sew the edges as you turn them under with your needle.

1 Beginning on a straight edge, use the tip of your needle to gently turn under the seam allowance about ½" at a time.

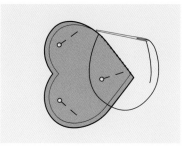

2 Using your nonsewing hand, hold the background and the turned seam allowance firmly between the thumb (on top) and forefinger (underneath) as you stitch the appliqué securely to the background fabric.

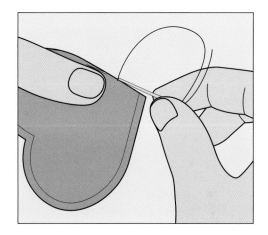

3 Stitch this ½" section to the background fabric, then needle turn the next ½" and repeat.

Welcome to Baltimore!

❀ ❀ ❀ ❀ ❀ ❀ ❀ ❀ ❀ ❀

Turning Neatly

A long milliner's or straw needle will help you control the seam allowance and turn it under neatly. A round wooden toothpick can also help you sweep the seam allowance under more easily.

Curves, points, stems, layered appliqué—all these elements require different techniques and stitches. Use this section to help you learn some specific techniques for appliquéing your Baltimore Album quilt.

Straight Edges

Straight edges are the easiest to appliqué, so this is a good place to concentrate on your basic appliqué stitches. Use the traditional appliqué stitch and try to keep your stitches straight, even, and consistent. Each stitch should be approximately ⅛" long.

Outside Curves

As you stitch around an outside curve, try to keep the appliqué edge smooth.

1. To keep little points of fabric from forming on the curves, push the seam allowance under with the tip of your needle, smoothing the folded edge before sewing. Keep your stitches a bit smaller so that these fabric points cannot escape between the stitches.

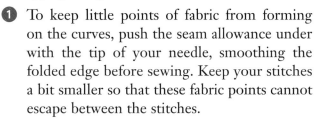

2. Remember, if your shape has sharp curves, refer to "Outside Curves" on page 42 to ease the excess fabric into a smooth curve. The basting really helps!

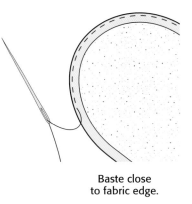

Baste close
to fabric edge.

Outside Points

As you stitch toward an outside point, take smaller stitches within ½" of the point. Smaller stitches near the point keep any frayed edges of the seam allowance from escaping.

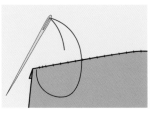

1. At the point, sew the last stitch on the first side of the piece very close to the point. Take one extra lock stitch in the exact same place before you switch sides at the point. This extra stitch will hold your fabric securely as you turn the point and adjust the fabric on the second side.

Lock stitch

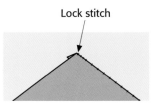

2 Before you stitch past the point, gently pull your thread in the direction of the point. This will accent the shape.

3 Place the next stitch on the opposite side of the point. A stitch on each side, close to the point, will accent the outside point. Don't put a stitch directly on the point because it might flatten the point.

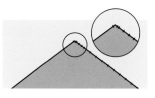

4 If a small tab of seam allowance extends beyond the edge of the appliqué, use your needle to push it under the appliqué before you stitch. Don't cut it off!

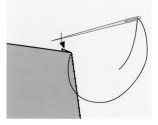

Inside Points

As you stitch toward an inside point (sometimes referred to as the cleavage), take smaller stitches within ½" of the point.

1 Stop stitching ¹⁄₁₆" before you get to the inside point.

2 Before you stitch the inside point, use your needle to sweep any loose threads under the point. Place the tip of your needle ½" past the point and gently sweep the needle back to the point, pushing any frayed threads under the appliqué. A round wooden toothpick used in place of the needle will also help you sweep any fuzzies under the appliqué.

Sweep tip of needle under appliqué and back toward inside point.

Welcome to Baltimore!

You're in Control!

A little dab of glue on your needle will control the fuzzies. Simply glide your needle over the top of your glue stick before you sweep the loose threads. This is my all-time favorite appliqué tip!

3 When you get to the deepest part of the point, use one large stitch to emphasize the point. Come up through the appliqué, catching a little more fabric in the stitch than normal—four or five threads from the fold instead of one or two. Make a straight stitch out over the edge of the appliqué, but insert your needle under the edge of the appliqué, pulling your needle through to the back. With the needle underneath, pull the needle toward you. This will enhance the cleavage at the point!

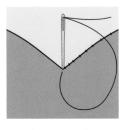

Insert needle
under appliqué edge.

4 If an inside point frays, use a few closely spaced stitches to tack the fabric down securely. If your thread matches the appliqué fabric, these stitches will blend in with the edge of the shape.

Inside Curves

The trick to appliquéing an inside curve is to clip the seam allowance.

1 An inside curve should be clipped in several places (every ¼") so that the seam allowance will relax and turn under smoothly. Clip only halfway through the seam allowance to avoid fraying at the edge of the appliqué.

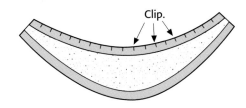

Clip.

2 If you're basting, use small stitches to hold the little pieces tight. If you're needle turning, use your needle to sweep the curve under before you appliqué.

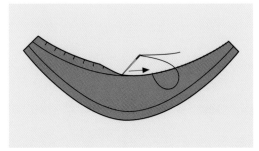

Shapes: Stems

After you've learned to appliqué the basic straight lines, curves, and points, you can apply those basics to shapes that appear in many of the Baltimore designs.

There are several methods for creating appliqué stems. If the stems are straight, they can be cut on the straight grain of the fabric. If stems curve, they must be cut on the bias.

STEM METHOD ONE

I love to use this method for stems, especially if they are curved.

1 Cut fabric strips that measure twice the finished stem width. For example, for a ¼" stem, cut the strips ½" wide. They can be cut easily with a rotary cutter, using a clear acrylic ruler as a guide.

2 Cut these strips into pieces ½" longer than the stem design on the pattern. This allows a ¼"-wide seam allowance at each end to be covered by leaves or flowers.

3 Fold both raw edges in to meet at the center, wrong sides together. Baste along the folded edges using small running stitches.

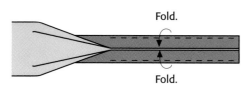

Fold.

Fold.

4 Position the strip on the marked stem line of your design, wrong side against the background fabric, and pin or baste the stem to the background fabric. Appliqué along both folded edges. When a stem is long, I like to glue it to the background fabric to keep it in place.

5 On a sharp curve, stitch the inside edge first, and then the outside edge. If you're making a curved stem or basket handle, pull gently on the inner basting thread and ease the fabric to create the curved stem.

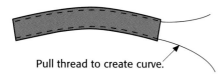

Pull thread to create curve.

6 Remove the basting threads after the stitching is complete.

7 You can also use a bias-tape maker to quickly make this kind of stem without basting. Spray your strips with spray starch and feed them into the wide end of the bias-tape maker. Press the folded stems as they emerge from the narrow end of the tool.

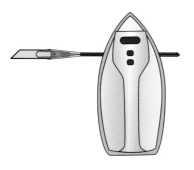

STEM METHOD TWO

I like to use this method for very thin stems.

1 Cut fabric strips that measure four times the finished stem width. For example, for a ⅛" stem, cut the strips ½" wide. They can be cut easily with a rotary cutter, using a clear acrylic ruler as a guide.

2 Cut these strips into pieces ½" longer than the stem design on the pattern. This allows a ¼"-wide seam allowance at each end to be covered by leaves or flowers.

3 Fold the strip in half lengthwise, wrong sides together. Press with a steam iron or baste close to the raw edges.

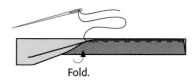

Fold.

4 Position the strip with the raw edges touching one of the marked stem lines. The folded edge of the stem should cover the other line. If the stems must curve, as in a wreath shape, position the raw edges of the strip just inside the outer curved line.

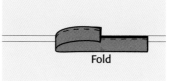

Fold

5 Using small running stitches, sew the strip to the background almost through the center of the strip, slightly closer to the raw edges than to the fold. Backstitch every few stitches to secure the stem to the background.

6 Roll the folded edge over the seam allowances. Appliqué the fold to the background fabric to create a smooth, thin stem.

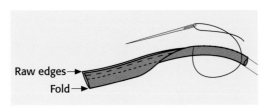

Raw edges →
Fold →

STEM METHOD THREE

You can use metal pressing bars, called bias bars, to make stems a uniform width. These are available at quilt shops in several sizes, from ⅛" to ½" wide. Choose the size that matches the *finished* width of the stems in your design.

1 Measure the width of the finished stem and cut bias strips of fabric twice this width plus ½" for seam allowances.

2 Fold the strip in half lengthwise, wrong sides together, and machine stitch a scant ¼" from the raw edges to make a tube. Slip the bias bar into the tube and position it with the seam centered on one side. Press the tube flat, with the seam allowance to one side. Be careful—the metal bars can get very hot. Push the bar through the tube to the other end. If necessary, trim the seam allowance so that it doesn't extend past the folded edge of the strip.

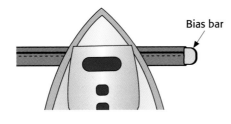

Bias bar

3 Remove the bar. Cut the tube into the required lengths for the stems (including seam allowances).

4 Position the stem on the background fabric with the seam allowance on the back. Pin or baste the stem to the background fabric and appliqué along both folded edges. On curved areas, stitch the inside curve in place first, and then the outside curve.

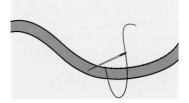

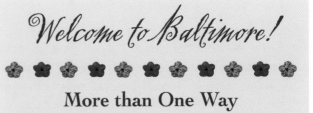

More than One Way

If you don't have bias bars, cut strips of heat-resistant template plastic or heavy paper (such as manila folders). You can make them any size and they work well!

Shapes: Leaves

Remember that the curved edges of leaves will be easy to baste and appliqué if the leaf is cut on the bias. The bias edge will ease along curves and create a smooth shape.

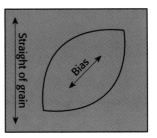

Straight of grain

Bias

- To shape leaves successfully, refer to the "Hand-Basting Primer" on page 41. Try the methods listed there to find what works best for you.

• At times, a leaf will be positioned under a flower or another leaf and become a partial leaf shape. For tips on working with overlapped pieces, refer to "Layered Appliqué" on page 56.

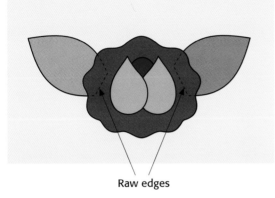

Raw edges

• If a leaf connects to a stem, begin stitching at the connection. Take one or two stitches from the leaf to the stem so that the pieces appear to be attached.

Shapes: Perfect Circles

I like to use heavy paper, such as a manila folder, to cut circular templates. You can also use heat-resistant template plastic. A plastic stencil with circles in multiple sizes, available at art stores, makes it easy to draw perfect shapes. Even better—you can find large paper punches in the scrapbooking area of your favorite craft store.

1 Place the plastic multicircle stencil over the circle in your appliqué pattern to find the correct finished size for your design. Trace the circle onto heavy paper. Cut out the paper circle template, cutting as slowly and smoothly as possible. Use small, sharp scissors for best results. You can use a nail file to smooth the paper edge if necessary.

2 Use the circle stencil again to trace a circle onto your fabric. Make this circle ½" larger in diameter than the paper circle. This adds a ¼"-wide seam allowance around the outer edge of the design. Cut out the fabric circle.

Wrong side of fabric

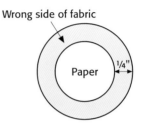

Paper ¼"

3 Using a small running stitch, sew within the seam allowance around the fabric circle, leaving at least 2" of thread at the beginning. Keep the stitches within the seam allowance, but not too close to the edge. Tie a single knot with the two thread ends and leave the thread ends loose.

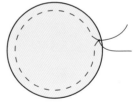

4 Place the paper template in the center of the fabric circle. Pull the thread ends to draw the seam allowance around the template. You can pin the circle to the pad of your ironing board with a big straight pin so that your hands will be free to pull the threads and adjust the fabric around the paper template.

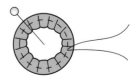

⑤ Steam press the fabric circle, using spray starch if you like, and then let it cool for a minute. Carefully peel back the fabric and remove the paper circle. Gently pull the basting threads to tighten the seam allowance again and make it lie flat. Tie another knot to secure the gathers, and trim the threads.

⑥ Pin the circle to the desired location on the background fabric and appliqué with smaller-than-usual stitches. For impressively small stitches, sew around the circle twice. The second time, place your stitches between the first ones.

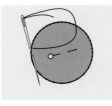

⑦ The paper templates that you remove before stitching are reusable. For larger circles, you can leave the paper inside the fabric until you've stitched the circle to the background. This helps to support the curves of the circle as you stitch. When you're finished, cut a slit in the background behind the circle and pull the paper out with tweezers. Your circles will be very smooth.

Welcome to Baltimore!

❀ ❀ ❀ ❀ ❀ ❀ ❀ ❀ ❀ ❀

Easy Circle Templates

You can also make circles by using self-stick dots, which are available in a variety of sizes at most office-supply stores. You can adhere them to the right side of your fabric, enabling you to needle-turn appliqué the circle to the background fabric.

Layered Appliqué

Many appliqué designs contain elements that are overlapped or layered. Here are some tips for completing these designs.

OVERLAPPED PIECES

If you look carefully at a design where two pieces touch, you'll notice that one piece looks like it overlaps the other. When you plan your stitching for projects in this book, refer to the numerical order as shown on the patterns.

Don't turn under and stitch the seam-allowance edges that will be covered by other pieces. As you appliqué, the raw edges of the first seam allowance will lie flat under the piece that covers it.

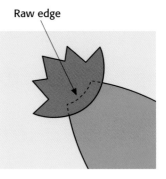

Raw edge

LAYERED ROSES

In addition to overlapping shapes, you'll also find roses with pieces that are layered on top of one another. When you appliqué the larger flower shape, the placement marks for the smaller petals disappear under the appliqué. An easy solution is to use a pattern overlay or simply make a window template for perfect placement of the petals.

❶ Trace the pieces of the flower pattern onto plain paper.

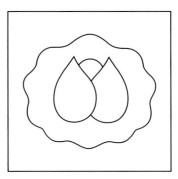

2 Cut out the larger flower shape, and then carefully cut out the petals to create a window.

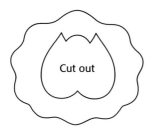

3 Place the paper window over the appliquéd flower piece. Position the petal pieces through the window for perfect placement.

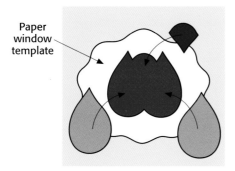

4 If you plan to quilt around the petals, it helps to trim away the background fabric behind the larger rose shape after you appliqué it. Leave a ¼"-wide seam allowance inside the appliqué stitches and then appliqué the petals on top.

Baskets

Make baskets with strips constructed using "Stem Method One" or "Stem Method Three" on pages 52–54. I like to use these methods because they allow you to actually weave the baskets.

1 Cut ½"-wide strips that measure ½" longer than the lines on the pattern, to allow a ¼" seam allowance. Prepare the strips.

2 Baste or glue the vertical strips to your background fabric but avoid placing stitches or glue where the horizontal basket lines cross.

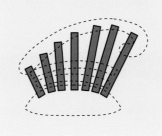

3 Weave the horizontal strips over and under the vertical strips. Raw edges of the horizontal strips should be tucked under the outer vertical strip. Appliqué the strips in place.

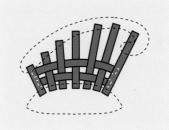

4 Appliqué the top and bottom of the basket, covering the raw edges of the strips. I like to use freezer paper under the fabric to baste the shapes.

5 To make the basket handle, use "Stem Method One" and baste the sides of the strip with small stitches. Gently pull the stitches on one side of the strip and ease the strip into a curve. Glue this in place and appliqué. I love this technique!

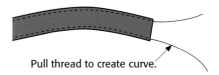

Pull thread to create curve.

Bows

Bows with three loops were often stitched onto antique Baltimore quilts. A dimensional effect can be created by using light and dark pieces of the same color. You can also use the right and wrong sides of a fabric. See the "Bow and Berry Wreath" block on page 76.

❶ Appliqué the right streamer first, then the side loops, and then the left streamer and center loop. Let the seam allowances extend into the center circle.

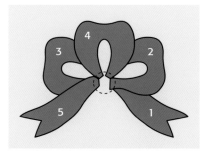

Welcome to Baltimore!

Needle Turn Inner Curves

It's difficult to baste the curves inside bow loops. Needle turn the curves under freezer paper placed on the top or back of your fabric. This will shape your fabric as you make small stitches around the curves.

❷ Cover the raw edges in the center with a perfect circle.

Birds

Birds are fun to appliqué in three pieces. Choose fabrics to simulate the texture of the bird's feathers.

❶ Appliqué the back wing first, letting the seam allowance extend under the body.

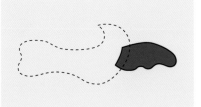

❷ Appliqué the body over the back wing.

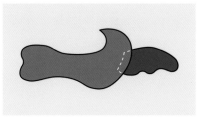

❸ Appliqué the front wing over the body.

❹ For the bird's eye, add a bead or an embroidered French knot.

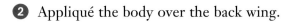
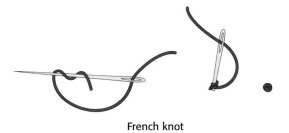

French knot

Once you've learned basic appliqué techniques, it's fun to add special touches with dimensional appliqué.

Folded Buds

1 Cut a 1¾" square of fabric. Fold the square in half diagonally, wrong sides together.

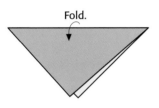

Fold.

2 Fold each side point down to the center point, overlapping the points so that they are about ¼" from the bottom point. Baste along the bottom edges of the bud.

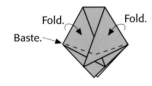

Fold.   Fold.

Baste.

3 Appliqué the calyx (base of the bud), leaving the top edge unstitched. Insert the bud into the calyx using tweezers. Appliqué the top of the calyx, taking a few stitches all the way through to the background to secure the bud. The top fold of the bud isn't stitched to the background.

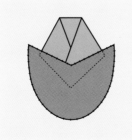

Gathered Blossoms

1 Cut a 2½"-diameter circle from fabric. Light-weight cottons work well for these flowers.

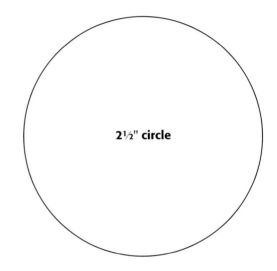

2½" circle

2 Turn under ⅛" around the edge of the circle and sew a running stitch near the fold. Use a double thread about 18" long.

3 Gather the edges in the center of the circle and tie a secure knot. If the edges don't meet tightly, take a few back-and-forth stitches at the center to close the hole.

④ Insert the needle straight down through the center of the gathers, bringing it through to the back (flat) side.

⑤ With the gathered side up, divide the circle into five equal flower petals as shown, marking lightly with a fabric marker.

⑥ To make the petals, bring the thread from the back over the outside edge of the flower (on the marked line) and insert it into the center again. Place the thread at one of the edge markings, then pull the thread to create a petal.

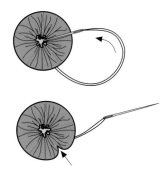

⑦ Continue looping the thread over the edges to make five petals. Knot the thread on the back of the flower but don't cut the thread. Add three beads to the flower center, and then tack the flower to the background fabric.

Gathered Flowers

Gathered flowers add a special touch to Baltimore appliqué designs. Using a technique known as ruching, you can create textured flowers with a variety of colors.

❶ Use a rotary cutter and ruler to cut a straight-grain strip of fabric 1⅛" wide and 30" long. With wrong sides together, fold the long edges of the strip toward the center so that the raw edges meet. Press.

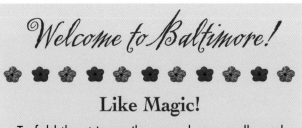
Fold.
Fold.

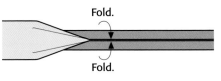

Welcome to Baltimore!

Like Magic!

To fold the strip easily, use a long needle and your ironing board. Take two stitches in your ironing board cover, leaving ½" (or your desired finished width) between the stitches and leaving the needle in place. Fold the strip of fabric as described in step 1 and thread it through the space. As you pull the strip under the needle, iron the folds to make a smooth strip. A steam iron and spray starch will help the strip hold its shape.

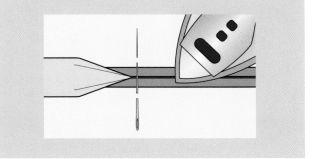

❷ Lay the folded strip right side up along the ruching guide on page 61. Use a fabric marker to place dots along both folded edges of your strip at 1" intervals. Mark the entire strip.

❸ Start ½" from one end with a secure knot and sew a zigzag running stitch from dot to dot. As you change directions, stitch over the folded edges.

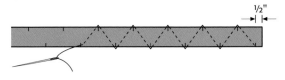
½"

4 Stitch about 6" before pulling the thread to gather the fabric. Pull the thread in a straight line, gathering fabric petals on each side. Stitch enough gathers to create at least 21 petals on each edge. Pull the gathering thread each time you change directions to prevent the thread from breaking.

5 Use a second needle and thread to form the flower. To begin, trim the beginning edge to ¼" and turn this seam allowance under the first petal. Tack it securely. Arrange the first five petals into a circle, and then take a stitch in each of these petals to draw them together. Take a stitch back into the first petal to form the center of your flower. Pull your thread to the back of your flower and tie a knot.

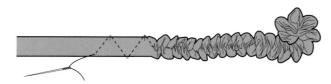

6 Carefully arrange the sixth and seventh petals slightly under the first one to begin making the second row of petals. Pin in place. Turn the flower over and tack the inside of the petals to the back as you form the flower.

7 When you get to the end of the flower, taper the last petal under the previous row, adjusting it to form a smooth shape. You may need to add a few petals. As you finish, your gathering stitches should stop on the outside edge of the strip. Pull the thread to make the last petal, and knot the thread. Cut the strip ¼" beyond the last stitch, then fold the raw edges under the flower.

8 After the flower is formed, start at the outside edge and appliqué the petals securely to the background fabric. Stitch the "tips" and "dips" of each petal. Your stitches will move in a spiral toward the center of the flower. When you get to the last petal at the flower center, stitch down the side of the petal to make it blend into the flower.

9 Add beads to the center of the flower.

Ruching guide for gathered flower

"Baltimore Basics" by Mimi Dietrich, 56" x 56"

I've designed 12 block patterns and appliqué lessons to go with them. The blocks fall into the following categories.

Square designs: Square designs look great when combined as a four-block album quilt and are also wonderful to use in the corners of a large quilt. Lessons 1 through 4 each feature a square-shaped block design.

Round designs: Wreath designs are traditional in Baltimore Album quilts. As you plan your quilt, place wreath patterns across from each other to balance your quilt design. Lessons 5 through 8 are round designs.

Fancy designs: Baltimore Album quilts are renowned for their fancy appliqué patterns. Baskets and vases full of flowers bring these quilts to life! Lessons 9 through 12 are examples of fancy designs.

Working through a Lesson

The stages required to complete each lesson are outlined below.

Step 1: Cut your background blocks. The Baltimore Basics patterns in this book are all printed full size, and the finished size of each block is 10" square. Normally, the background fabric would be cut 10½" square to include ¼"-wide seam allowances on all sides. However, because appliqué blocks sometimes fray or distort during stitching, I like to cut the squares 1" larger (11½" x 11½") and then trim them to the correct size (10½" x 10½") after I've completed the appliqué. You can accurately cut the blocks by using a rotary cutter, mat, and acrylic ruler. Refer to "Cutting Background Fabric" on page 32.

Step 2: Transfer the appliqué pattern. Referring to "Marking Appliqué Placement Lines" on page 32, fold the fabric in quarters and trace the appliqué design onto the background fabric.

Fold

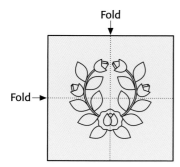

Fold→

If you're planning a quilt with a diagonal setting, fold the fabric in quarters diagonally when tracing wreaths, baskets, and vases. You can also use a pattern overlay.

Fold

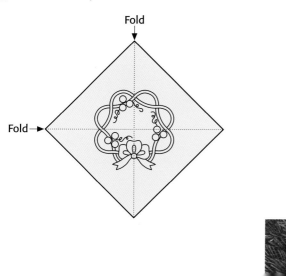

Fold→

Step 3: Make templates. Trace the appliqué patterns onto freezer paper or template plastic. Refer to "Making Templates and Cutting Appliqué Pieces" on page 34.

Step 4: Prepare the appliqué pieces. Using your favorite method, get the appliqué pieces ready for stitching. Refer to "Preparing Appliqué Pieces" on page 38.

Step 5: Stitch the appliqués in place. You'll find an appliqué stitching sequence with each pattern. The numbered steps refer to the numbered pattern pieces.

Welcome to Baltimore!

Making an Album Quilt

Below are some ideas to help you create a wonderful album quilt—or two!

- Make a block each month and by this time next year you'll have enough blocks for a Baltimore quilt.
- Work on all the blocks at once! Stitch one technique or shape each month: stems, leaves, hearts, circles, vases, baskets, buds, layered roses, gathered blossoms, gathered flowers, birds, and bows.
- Try different appliqué methods and collect blocks for a large quilt, or make a few four-block quilts.

Crossed Leaves

Trace the design onto your background fabric, and then appliqué the pieces in the following order.

1. Cut two strips, ½" x 7½". Appliqué the two stems using "Stem Method One" on page 52.

2. Cut 20 freezer-paper leaves and prepare your appliqués using "Method Two: Freezer Paper on Back—Basted Preparation" on page 38.

This method will keep the shapes of your leaves consistent and you'll be a leaf expert when you're finished!

3. Cut four ⅝" circles from heavy paper and four 1⅛" fabric circles. Make "Perfect Circles," referring to page 55.

Crossed Leaves

Oak Reel

Trace the design onto your background fabric, or try a pattern overlay for appliqué placement. Appliqué the pieces in the following order.

❶ Cut one center shape from freezer paper and prepare your appliqué using "Method Two: Freezer Paper on Back—Basted Preparation" on page 38. Clip the inside curves to help them turn smoothly.

❷ Cut four curves using freezer paper on the back of your fabric and appliqué them around the center. Don't forget to clip the inside curves.

❸ Prepare four oak leaves using freezer paper on the back of your fabric. Use a glue stick to control the curves on the leaves. Appliqué with little stitches as you sew the inside curves on the leaves.

❹ Cut sixteen ⅝" circles from heavy paper and sixteen 1⅛" fabric circles. Make "Perfect Circles," referring to page 55.

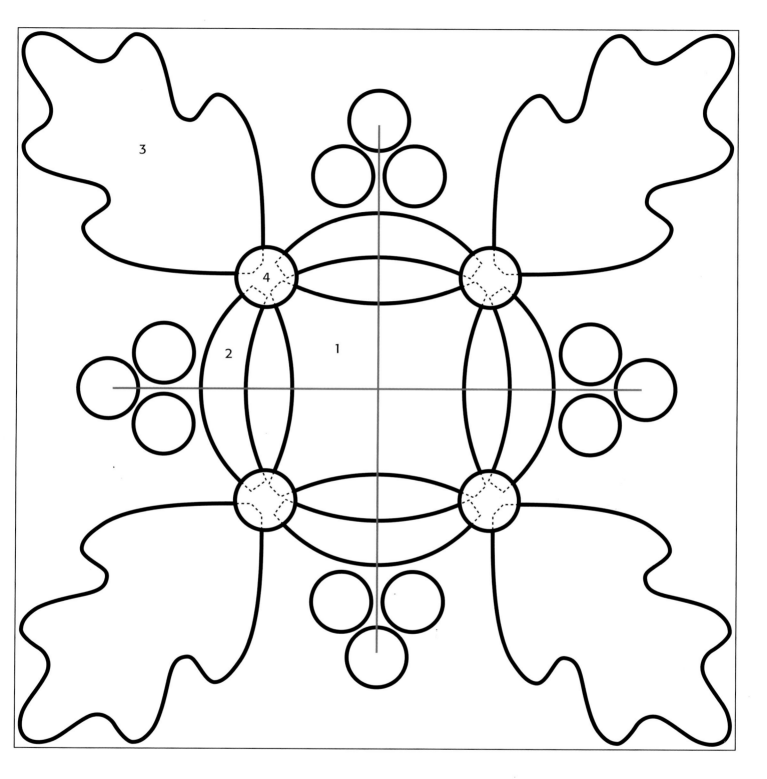

Oak Reel

Pineapples

Instead of tracing the design onto the background or using a pattern overlay, try marking the back of the background fabric and using the technique described in "Method Four: Stitch-Marked Appliqué Preparation" on page 40. This method will help keep all of the pieces perfectly placed. Appliqué the pieces in the following order.

❶ Appliqué the four pineapples using needle-turn appliqué. The seam allowances should extend past the lines of the leaves and tops; baste these seam allowances so that they stay in place.

❷ Appliqué the leaves, clipping the inside curves as you needle turn the edges.

❸ Appliqué the pineapple tops, clipping the inside points and using little stitches to control the points.

❹ Cut eight ⅝" circles from heavy paper and eight 1⅛" fabric circles. Make "Perfect Circles," referring to page 55.

Pineapples

 LESSON 4

Blooming Buds

This is a great design for combining the lessons you've already learned. Mark the center design on the back of your background fabric. Turn the fabric over and mark the stems, buds, and circles on the right side of the fabric. Appliqué the pieces in the following order.

❶ Cut four ½" x 2½" bias strips and eight ½" x 1½" bias strips. Appliqué the stems using "Stem Method Two" on page 53.

❷ Prepare the center design using "Method Four: Stitch-Marked Appliqué Preparation"

on page 40. Use needle-turn appliqué to stitch the design. Here's a word of advice—be careful when you cut out the square in the center!

❸ Appliqué the folded buds using the directions on page 59.

❹ Cut eight ½" circles from heavy paper and eight 1" circles from fabric. Make "Perfect Circles," referring to page 55. These are a little smaller than the circles in the previous lessons—you can do it!

Blooming Buds

Rose Wreath

Trace the design onto your background fabric and then appliqué the pieces in the following order.

❶ Cut two bias strips, ½" x 6½". Appliqué the stems using "Stem Method Two" on page 53. Be careful not to stretch the stems as you sew.

❷ Cut 12 freezer-paper leaves and prepare your appliqués using "Method Two: Freezer Paper on Back—Basted Preparation" on page 38. This method will keep the shapes of your leaves consistent.

❸ Appliqué the four buds using the directions on page 59.

❹ Appliqué the layered rose using the directions on page 56.

Design variation: Substitute a gathered flower for the layered rose; substitute gathered blossoms for the buds.

Rose Wreath

Cherry Wreath

This is a great design for combining lessons you've already learned. Mark the center circle design on the back of your background fabric. Turn the fabric over and mark the stems and circles on the right side of the fabric. Appliqué the pieces in the following order.

1 Prepare the center circle using "Method Four: Stitch-Marked Appliqué Preparation" on page 40. Use needle-turn appliqué to stitch the circle. One word of advice—be careful when you cut out the center!

2 Cut 12 freezer-paper leaves and prepare your appliqués using "Method Two: Freezer Paper on Back—Basted Preparation" on page 38. This method will keep the shapes of your leaves consistent.

3 Appliqué the twelve ⅝" berries, referring to "Perfect Circles" on page 55.

4 Use a fine-line permanent marker to ink the thin stems, or use an embroidered stem stitch.

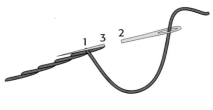

Outline or stem stitch

Design variation: Substitute buds or gathered blossoms for the berries on the outside of the wreath.

Cherry Wreath
* Design variation

Bow and Berry Wreath

Trace the design onto your background fabric. Appliqué the pieces in the following order.

1. Cut two bias strips, ½" x 6½". Appliqué the two stems using "Stem Method One" on page 52. Pull gently on one of the basting threads to create the curved stems.

2. Cut 10 freezer-paper leaves and prepare your appliqués using "Method Two: Freezer Paper on Back—Basted Preparation" on page 38. This method will keep the shapes of your leaves consistent.

3. Appliqué the twelve ⅝" berries, referring to "Perfect Circles" on page 55.

4. Appliqué the bow using the directions in "Bows" on page 58.

Design variation: Substitute gathered blossoms for the berries on the wreath.

Bow and Berry Wreath

Grapevine Wreath

Trace the design onto your background fabric. Appliqué the pieces in the following order.

1 Cut two bias strips, ½" x 19". Appliqué the two stems using "Stem Method One" on page 52. Working with both prepared stems, use a glue stick to baste the stems to the background fabric, weaving them over and under each other.

2 Appliqué nine ⅝" berries, referring to "Perfect Circles" on page 55.

3 Appliqué the bow using the directions in "Bows" on page 58.

4 Use a fine-line permanent marker to ink the tendrils, or use an embroidered stem stitch.

Design variation: Substitute gathered blossoms for the grapes on the wreath.

Grapevine Wreath

Straight Vase

Trace the design onto your background fabric, or try a pattern overlay for appliqué placement. Appliqué the pieces in the following order.

1. Cut two bias strips, ½" x 1½". Appliqué the stems using "Stem Method Two" on page 53.

2. Use freezer paper on the back of your fabric to shape and appliqué the vase.

3. Appliqué two ⅞" circles on the top of the vase, referring to "Perfect Circles" on page 55.

4. Cut six freezer-paper leaves and prepare your appliqués, referring to "Method Two: Freezer Paper on Back—Basted Preparation" on page 38.

5. Appliqué the heart, referring to "Hand-Basting Primer" on page 41.

6. Appliqué the two buds using the directions on page 59.

7. Appliqué the layered rose using the directions on page 56.

8. Appliqué the bird using the directions on page 58.

9. Add dimensional appliqué to your block using the directions in "Gathered Flowers" on page 60.

10. Appliqué four gathered blossoms using the directions on page 59.

Straight Vase

Curved Vase

Trace the design onto your background fabric or try a pattern overlay for appliqué placement. Appliqué the pieces in the following order.

❶ Cut two bias strips, ½" x 1½". Appliqué the stems using "Stem Method Two" on page 53.

❷ Cut six freezer-paper leaves and prepare your appliqués using "Method Two: Freezer Paper on Back—Basted Preparation" on page 38. The two partial leaves are layered under the vase.

❸ Use freezer paper on the back of your fabric to shape and appliqué the vase.

❹ Appliqué the heart using "Hand-Basting Primer" on page 41.

❺ Appliqué the two buds using the directions on page 59.

❻ Appliqué the layered rose using the directions on page 56.

❼ Appliqué the bird using the directions on page 58.

❽ Add dimensional appliqué to your block using the directions in "Gathered Flowers" on page 60.

❾ Appliqué four gathered blossoms using the directions on page 59.

Curved Vase

Straight Basket

Trace the design onto your background fabric, or try a pattern overlay for appliqué placement. Appliqué the pieces in the following order.

1. Cut one bias strip, ½" x 12½". Appliqué the basket handle using "Stem Method One" on page 52. Pull gently on one of the basting threads to create the curved stems.

2. Cut seven strips, ½" x 2½". Appliqué the vertical basket strips using "Stem Method One" on page 52.

3. Use freezer paper on the back of your fabric to appliqué the top and bottom of the basket. Use the basting method on page 42 to shape the curved ends.

4. Cut six freezer-paper leaves and prepare your appliqués using "Method Two: Freezer Paper on Back—Basted Preparation" on page 38.

5. Appliqué the heart using "Hand-Basting Primer" on page 41.

6. Appliqué the two buds using the directions on page 59.

7. Appliqué the layered rose using the directions on page 56.

8. Add dimensional appliqué to your block using the directions in "Gathered Flowers" on page 60.

9. Appliqué four gathered blossoms using the directions on page 59.

Straight Basket

Curved Basket

Trace the design onto your background fabric, or try a pattern overlay for appliqué placement. Appliqué the pieces in the following order.

1 Cut one bias strip, ½" x 13". Appliqué the basket handle using "Stem Method One" on page 52. Pull gently on one of the basting threads to create the curved handle.

2 Cut nine bias strips, ½" x 3½". Trim the strips to match the pieces on the pattern and follow the directions for weaving the basket on page 57. Use "Stem Method One" on page 52.

3 Cut one bias strip, ½" x 2". Appliqué the bud stem using "Stem Method Two" on page 53.

4 Use freezer paper on the back of your fabric to appliqué the top and bottom of the basket.

5 Cut six freezer-paper leaves and prepare your appliqués using "Method Two: Freezer Paper on Back—Basted Preparation" on page 38.

6 Appliqué the heart using "Hand-Basting Primer" on page 41.

7 Appliqué the two buds using the directions on page 59.

8 Appliqué the layered rose using the directions on page 56.

9 Add dimensional appliqué to your block using the directions in "Gathered Flowers" on page 60.

10 Appliqué four gathered blossoms using the directions on page 59.

Curved Basket

Many stitchers love to appliqué and collect Baltimore blocks. However, when it comes to finishing the quilt, I discovered that some of my students had never squared up their blocks or measured the pieced top before attaching borders. This is one of the main reasons I wanted to write this book! Here are all the basics you need to finish your quilt.

Washing the Blocks

Always wash your blocks when you finish stitching. This removes any pencil marks and finger smudges. Simply run warm water in the sink with some mild soap. Place the block in the water and soak it for a while, then rinse it with water until there are no more soap bubbles. Don't wrinkle it or wring it dry. Place the block, right side down, on a clean towel. Roll it up to get most of the moisture out, then unroll it and let it dry flat.

If any colors run, wash the block again, scrubbing the area with a clean toothbrush and mild soap if necessary. Rinse.

Press the back of the block with a steam iron. Now it's clean and neat and ready to be squared up before you sew it into your quilt.

Squaring Up Blocks

Before you stitch your blocks together, trim them to size and square up the blocks, keeping the design centered.

Here are some ideas for squaring up the blocks.

- Using a large square acrylic ruler, line up the centerlines (folds) of the block design on the background fabric with the centerlines of the desired square size on the ruler. The centerline of the 10½" square block design is the 5¼" line on the ruler. Cut the first two sides

of the block using a sharp rotary cutter. Turn the block around, matching the cut edges to the 10½" lines, and cut the other two sides.

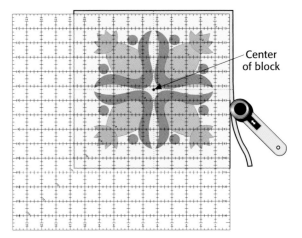

Center of block

- Cut a 10½" square piece of template plastic. Mark the horizontal, vertical, and diagonal centerlines on the plastic. Place the plastic over your appliquéd block, using the lines to center the design. Draw around the edges, and then cut with scissors or a rotary cutter.

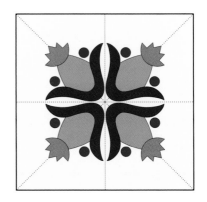

- You can also go to a frame store and purchase a 16"-square picture mat with an opening the size of your finished block plus the seam allowance (10½"). Place the mat over the block and center the appliquéd design in the opening. Draw around the inside edge, and then cut with scissors or a rotary cutter. This works great for blocks with dimensional appliqué.

Rotary Cutting

You can cut sashing strips, borders, and binding strips easily with a rotary cutter, mat, and acrylic ruler. Please note that the following instructions are written for right-handed quilters. If you're left-handed, reverse the placement of the ruler and rotary cutter shown in the illustrations.

1 To straighten the fabric for accurate cutting, press your fabric and fold it in half lengthwise with the selvages parallel. Fold the fabric again, bringing the fold up to match the selvages. Place the fabric on the cutting mat.

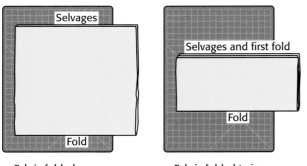

Fabric folded once   Fabric folded twice

2 Place a small square ruler (I like to use a 6" square) on the fold nearest you, aligning it with the folded edge. Place a larger ruler (I like 4" x 18" or 6" x 12") next to the square so that it covers the uneven edge of the fabric.

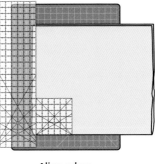

Align rulers.

3 Holding the long ruler, remove the small square ruler and make a clean cut along the edge of the long ruler. Roll the rotary cutter away from you using firm pressure on both the ruler and the rotary cutter.

Make a clean cut.

4 To cut strips, align the clean-cut edge of the fabric with the ruler marking for the desired strip width and cut a strip. Cut smaller pieces by turning the strip and trimming the end. Again, align the clean-cut edge of the strip with the ruler marking for the desired size and cut.

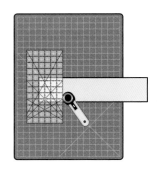

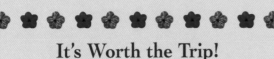

Welcome to Baltimore!

It's Worth the Trip!

If your rotary cutter has a dull blade, it may skip spots as you run it along your fabric. Head to the store and buy a new blade—or a new cutter. It's amazing how a sharp blade improves your cutting.

Sewing Accurate Seams

One of the most important skills for a quilter to master is sewing accurate ¼" seam allowances. Many machines have a presser foot that measures ¼" from the stitching line to the right side of the foot. Test your machine by sewing a sample seam, guiding the cut edge of your fabric into your machine just under the right edge of the foot. If it is wider or narrower than ¼", adjust how you guide your fabric so that the seam will measure ¼". If you don't have a ¼" presser foot, you can make a guide by placing a piece of masking tape on your machine in front of the presser foot.

← Masking tape

¼"

Pressing Seams

When I sew blocks together without any sashing, I press the seams open. This distributes the seam "shadows" on light-colored backgrounds and distributes the thickness of the seam allowance when I hand quilt.

When I sew blocks together with sashing, I press the seams toward the sashing strips. This eliminates the seam shadows and makes it easy to hand quilt along the edge of the block. I press the border seams toward the borders.

Sashing

Some quilters like their blocks set side by side in the quilt, while others like the way sashing between the blocks frames each individual block. You can determine your own preferences by doing advance research about various quilt styles.

Here are a few tips for deciding if you want to use sashing in your quilt.

- Lay out your blocks and take a photo. Make two copies. Use a marker to draw lines between the blocks on one photo, but leave the other plain. You'll probably like one more than the other.

- To help you decide which fabric to use for sashing, lay a piece of fabric on a flat surface. Place the blocks on top of the fabric, leaving 1" spaces between the blocks. Audition fabrics until you find the best one. I like 1"-wide sashing. It frames the individual blocks, but the narrow strips don't require quilting.

- Some quilters also like sashing squares where the sashing intersects. This is a great place for an accent fabric or your "inspiration" fabric. Sashing squares are cut the same raw size as the width of the sashing strips. Simply count the number of sashing intersections in your quilt plan to determine how many squares you'll need. Instead of long horizontal sashing strips, all the sashing strips will be cut the raw size of the blocks.

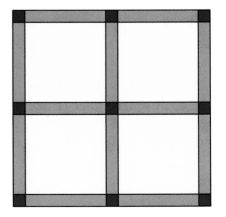

Straight Settings

In straight sets, blocks are laid out in horizontal rows. Lay the blocks out on a flat surface. Sew the blocks together into rows, and then join the rows to complete the middle of the quilt.

STRAIGHT SETTINGS WITH SASHING

① Lay the blocks out on a flat surface.

② Cut the number of 1½" x 10½" vertical sashing strips as indicated in the setting directions. Place them between the blocks.

③ Sew the blocks and strips together into rows. Press toward the sashing strips.

④ Cut the horizontal sashing strips 1½" x the measurement listed in the setting directions.

Welcome to Baltimore!

Setting a Deadline

Often when I have a decision to make about a quilt setting, I lay out the blocks on a table. As I walk by the table, I make changes. I always give myself a deadline—like Friday at 5:00 p.m. Whatever is on the table at the deadline is my final decision.

Cutting Long Setting Strips

I'm an appliqué person, and I'm not always precise when piecing my quilt. (I'll admit it!) I cut my long setting strips and borders at least 2" longer than the pattern measurements. When I'm ready to sew the strips to my quilt, I trim them to match my quilt. Sometimes I use a tape measure, but more often I just lay the strips over the center of the pieced blocks and cut the strips to match.

⑤ Sew the block rows together with the horizontal sashing strips. Press toward the sashing strips.

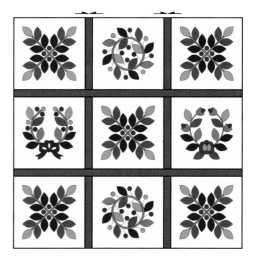

If you're using sashing squares, sew them into long rows with the sashing strips. Press toward the sashing strips.

Diagonal Settings

Quilts with blocks set on point are constructed in diagonal rows, with setting triangles added around the edges to complete the corners and sides of the quilt. Arrange the blocks and setting triangles in diagonal rows on a flat surface before you start sewing. Make sure that all the blocks are the same size and absolutely square. Pick up and sew one row at a time, and then join the rows to complete the quilt.

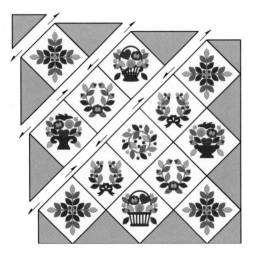

To insert sashing strips in a diagonally set quilt, lay the blocks out on a flat surface as shown. Place the short sashing strips between the blocks.

Sew the blocks and strips together into rows. After you sew the rows together, sew the longer sashing strips between the rows.

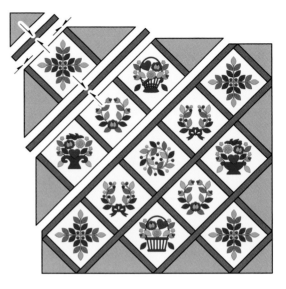

If you're using sashing squares, sew them into long rows with the sashing strips. Press toward the sashing strips.

After the blocks have been sewn together, you can add a border to frame them. Following are suggestions for different styles of quilt borders.

Inner Borders

Inner borders will frame your appliquéd blocks and accent the outer borders. I love to use inner borders that finish at 1" wide because the narrow strips do not require quilting. You can adjust the sizes given in the patterns and cut wider borders, or you can also omit the inner borders completely. It's your quilt!

Sew the inner borders to your quilt, referring to "Borders with Simple Corners" on page 96.

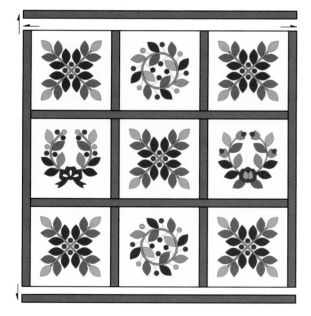

Basic Borders

You can finish the edges of your quilt beautifully by adding basic fabric borders. The border sizes given in the various quilt-setting options are for basic borders. If you started your quilt with an inspiration fabric, this will make a fabulous border.

My "Baltimore Basics" quilt on page 62 has basic borders. I wanted to let my students know that it's perfectly OK to finish a Baltimore quilt this way. The floral fabric is perfect, and using this type of border means that the quilt is finished sooner than later. Sew the outer border around your quilt, referring to "Borders with Mitered Corners" on page 97.

Welcome to Baltimore!

❁ ❁ ❁ ❁ ❁ ❁ ❁ ❁ ❁ ❁

Simply Speaking

One of my students called me several years after she had finished the blocks for her quilt, looking for ideas for her border. I simply asked her if she still had the floral inspiration fabric. She had 3 yards, and the quilt top was finished the following week!

Appliquéd Borders

Using appliquéd borders on a Baltimore quilt is like putting frosting on a cake! They give the quilt a special touch. I like to appliqué the borders separately from the quilt before I sew them to the edges. It's so much easier to appliqué a border strip without handling the entire quilt. Most appliquéd borders use the same background fabric that was used for the blocks.

❶ Don't start the borders until the quilt center is completed. You might change your mind!

❷ If your quilt is square, photocopy enough border and corner pattern pieces for one side of your quilt. If your quilt is rectangular, photocopy enough border and corner pattern pieces for one short and one long side of your quilt. Tape the copies together so that you have a pattern for either one or both (length and width) sides. Mark the center of the border and corner patterns.

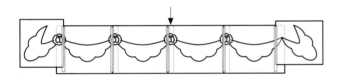

❸ Place this pattern next to your quilt, matching the quilt center and the border-pattern center, making sure the border will fit the edge of your quilt. Sometimes you need to fudge a little—adjust the placement of some of the pieces to make it fit. If you have added sashing strips between your blocks, you'll need to space the swag or vine patterns 1" apart on your border. These spaces will eventually be covered by an appliquéd motif.

❹ When you're sure that the border fits your quilt, trace the border design onto the background fabric for your border strips and start to appliqué. Mark the center of your border strips, because you'll need these marks to sew the borders to your quilt later.

Double-Checking

If you want to be perfectly sure the borders fit the quilt, baste the borders onto the edges of your quilt with large stitches. Mark the appliqué placement lines so that you're sure they fit, and then remove the borders to stitch the appliqué.

❺ Repeat fabrics used in your quilt for the appliquéd border. Your inspiration fabric is perfect for swags. Appliqué fabrics that are left over from the center of the quilt are great for flowers, buds, hearts, and leaves. Prepare your appliqué pieces using your favorite technique.

❻ Appliqué all motifs on the border strips except the corners, referring to "Swag Borders" below or "Vine Borders" on page 95. Finish appliquéing the corners *after* the borders are stitched to the quilt and mitered. On swag borders, appliqué the corner swag and two flowers last. For a vine border, connect the corner vines with a flower.

SWAG BORDERS

My favorite borders for appliquéd quilts are appliquéd swags. There's just something happy about this type of design that always appeals to me.

● Swags can be combined with layered roses, gathered flowers, hearts, or bows. The pattern in this book features roses, but you can easily substitute another appliquéd shape.

- You can also change the swags by smoothing out the scallops or dividing the swag into sections to make double or triple swags.

- To make the pattern for a swag border, cut a long piece of freezer paper the size of the border strips given for the quilt setting that you chose. Trace the swags and any decorative motifs (such as roses) on the freezer paper so that you can see what the finished border will look like. The swag border pattern on pages 98–99 has a 10" repeat to match the finished block size. Remember, if you're using sashing strips in your quilt, you need to space the swags apart by 1" (the width of the sashing).

Transfer the pattern to the border background. Make templates and prepare the appliqué pieces using your favorite technique. Stitch the appliqués to the border background, reserving the corner swags and adjacent flowers. Appliqué them to the quilt after the borders are stitched to the quilt and mitered.

VINE BORDERS

Many quilters like appliquéd borders with vines that curve around the edges of the quilt. It's easy to design these borders if you use the following elements to make the vine.

1 Start by cutting a paper rectangle the length of one of your blocks and the width of your border. For the quilts in this book, that would be 6" x 10".

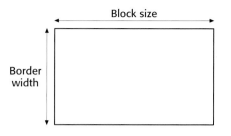

2 Divide the rectangle into 16 sections and draw a curved line as shown. This unit will be repeated around the sides of your quilt.

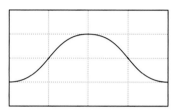

To make the pattern for a vine border, cut a long piece of freezer paper the size of the border given for the quilt setting that you chose. Trace the vines repeatedly on the freezer paper so that you can see what the finished border will look like. If you're using sashing strips in your quilt, you need to space the vine sections apart by 1" (the width of the sashing) and then draw a line to connect the sections.

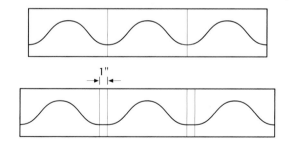

3 For the corner, start with a square the size of your border width. For the quilts in this book, you need a 6" square. Place this square next to your vine pattern and continue drawing the vine to make the corner, such as in the sample shown here. You will find vine border patterns on pages 100–101.

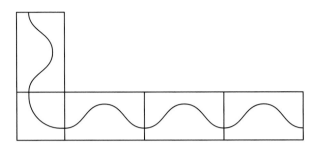

4 Transfer the pattern to the border background strips. Make templates and prepare the appliqué pieces using your favorite techniques. To make the vine, measure the length of the vine that you will need. Use green fabric from your quilt appliqués and cut enough ½"-wide bias strips to make the vine. Using "Stem Method One" on page 52, appliqué the vine. You can appliqué it in one continuous piece by sewing smaller strips together, or you can appliqué short strips between flowers or other motifs. To complete the vine, add leaves, flowers, hearts, berries, blossoms, or other designs from your blocks.

APPLIQUÉD BORDER CORNERS

If you don't want a vine around the entire quilt, try appliquéd corners on your border. Use them in opposite corners or in all four corners of the quilt. Select your favorite appliqué motifs from those used in the block patterns. Below are two ideas for combining motifs into corner designs.

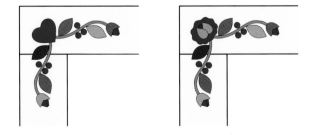

Measuring for Borders

While various quilt-setting options in this book provide specific border measurements, I recommend that you measure your quilt before attaching borders. Because of stitching variations, your assembled quilt top may vary in size from the pattern measurements, so it's always a good idea to check the actual measurements of your quilt.

Always measure a quilt through its center in both directions. Center measurements are most accurate because the edges of the quilt may have stretched during assembly. If necessary, trim the length of your inner borders to match the quilt size. Careful measuring will prevent ripples and result in smooth, even borders on your quilt.

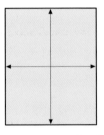

Measure center of quilt.

Borders with Simple Corners

Borders with simple corners are easy to sew to a quilt. I always use this method for narrow borders that are 1" wide or less. I also use this method when I just want a quick-and-easy border, no matter how wide the borders may be. The inner borders of the quilts in this book use this type of border.

1 Fold the quilt in half in both directions and mark the center of each side with a pin. Fold each border strip in half crosswise and mark the center with a pin. Match the center of a side border to the center of one side of your quilt and pin. Match the cut ends of the border to the raw ends of the quilt and pin. Continue to pin together, easing the edge of the quilt to fit the border if necessary.

② Sew the side border strip to the quilt. Press seams toward the border. Repeat for the other side.

③ Using the same process, sew the top and bottom border strips to the quilt, overlapping the two side borders. Press the seams toward the border.

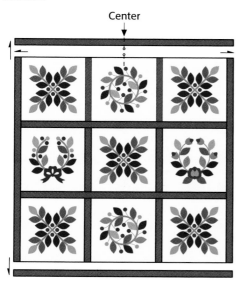

Center

Borders with Mitered Corners

I like to miter the corners of the outer borders on my Baltimore quilts. There are several ways to sew mitered corners, but this is my favorite method because it always results in square corners. Note: The border measurements provided in each set of project instructions include an extra 2" to help you miter your corners accurately.

① Sew the border strips to the quilt top, beginning and ending ¼" from the raw edges of the quilt top. Press the seams toward the borders.

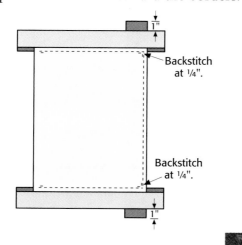

1"

Backstitch at ¼".

Backstitch at ¼".

1"

② To miter a corner, lay a corner of the quilt top on a flat surface. Fold the vertical border strip under at a 45° angle against the adjacent border. Use a square ruler to check that the corner is flat and square. Press the fold to crease it.

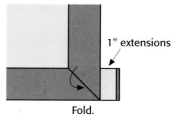

1" extensions

Fold.

③ Carefully center a piece of 1"-wide masking tape over the mitered fold. The tape will hold your miter in place while you sew the bias seam.

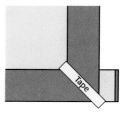

Tape

④ Turn down the vertical border, folding the quilt diagonally. Use a pencil to draw a line on the crease on the wrong side of the border.

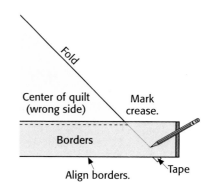

Fold

Center of quilt (wrong side)

Mark crease.

Borders

Align borders.

Tape

5 Stitch on the pencil line, through the two borders, being careful not to sew through the tape. Remove the tape.

meet. Cut away the excess fabric, leaving a ¼" seam, and press the seam open. Repeat for the other three corners.

Stitch.

¼" seam allowance

Trim.

6 Make sure the seam lies flat on the quilt front and that there are no pleats or puckers in the corner where the borders and the quilt top

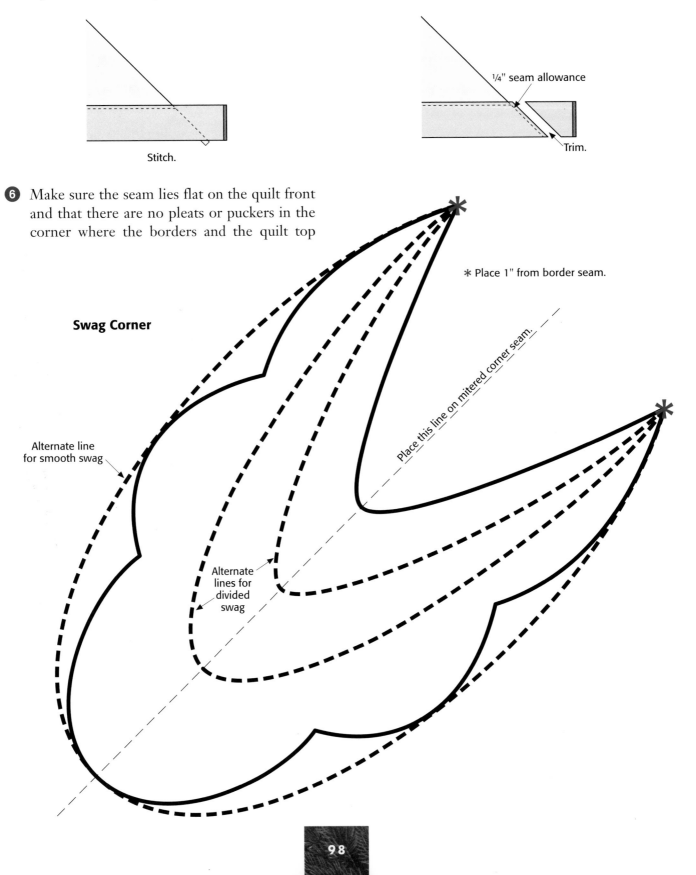

✳ Place 1" from border seam.

Place this line on mitered corner seam.

Swag Corner

Alternate line for smooth swag

Alternate lines for divided swag

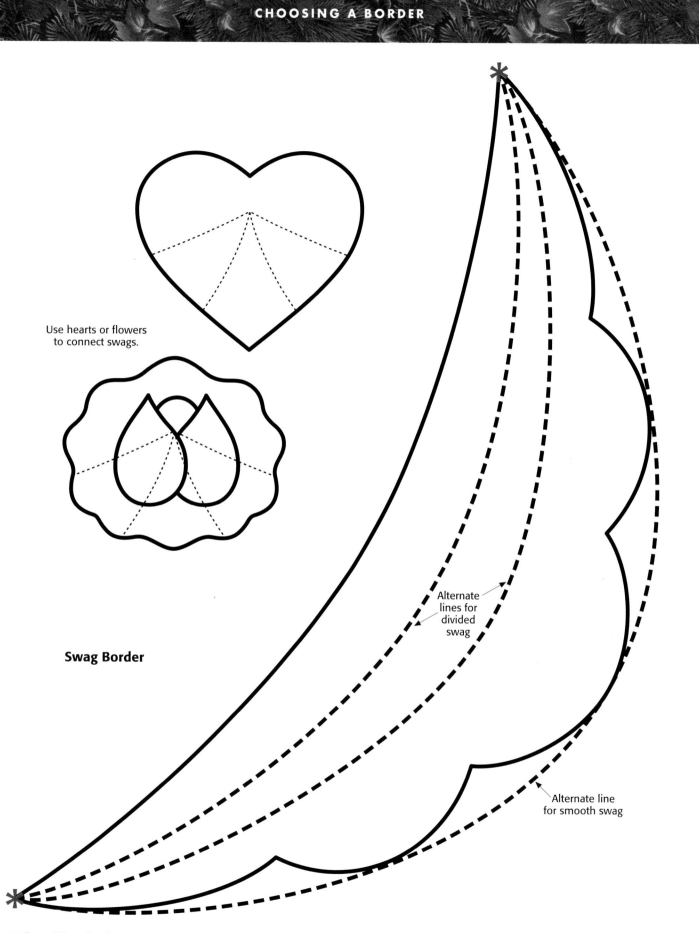

Use hearts or flowers
to connect swags.

Swag Border

Alternate
lines for
divided
swag

Alternate line
for smooth swag

✳ Place 1" from border seam.

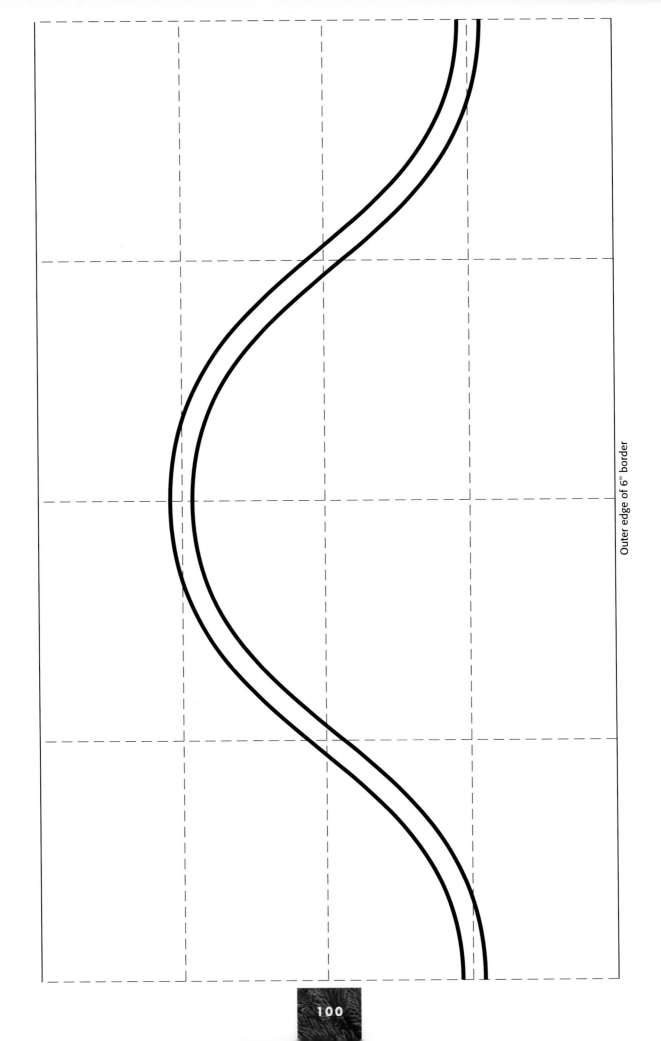

Outer edge of 6" border

Mitered seam

Outer edge of 6" border

Outer edge of 6" border

After you've completed your Baltimore Album top, it's time to quilt your masterpiece. Your quilting stitches will outline and define your appliqué pieces. They can also create a design in the background area that adds a wonderful texture to your quilt.

Hand-quilting stitches are short running stitches used to hold the top, batting, and backing of your quilt together. For hand quilting, a lightweight batting will provide a traditional look while helping your needle glide easily through the layers.

Traditionally, appliquéd quilts are quilted with two kinds of quilting. The first outlines the appliqué pieces. The stitches lie just outside the appliqué, adding dimension and definition to the appliqué pieces. The stitches go through the background of the quilt, batting, and backing, just outside the appliqué edges. Many appliqué pieces will appear to be stuffed after this quilting has been completed.

Quilting stitches can outline shapes within an appliqué design, such as the petals of a rose. In this case, the quilting stitches go through part of the appliqués as well as the other layers of the quilt.

The second kind of quilting is background quilting. Straight lines or other repetitive designs are stitched through the background fabric, batting, and backing. Background quilting doesn't usually continue through the appliqués.

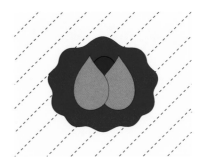

Marking the Quilting Design

Mark the quilting designs after constructing the quilt top and before basting the three layers of the quilt together. Lay the quilt flat while marking it so that the lines will be smooth and accurate.

You can use a variety of tools to mark the quilting design onto the quilt top: a mechanical pencil, a silver marking pencil, a water-soluble pen, or a light-colored chalk pencil for dark fabrics. Whichever marking tool you use, test the tool on a scrap of your background fabric before using it on your quilt. Make sure you can see the lines and that you can remove them.

To mark a specific quilting design, place the quilt top on top of the quilting pattern and trace the design onto the fabric. If you find it difficult to see the lines of the pattern, first trace over the lines of the pattern using a dark felt-tip marker. If you still have difficulty, you can place the pattern on a light box with the quilt on top. You should be able to see the marks through the fabric. Refer to "Homemade Light Box" on page 33 to see how you can create a light box using your dining-room table. You can also use a quilting stencil by placing it on top of the quilt.

DIAGONAL LINES

Among many hand quilters, it's traditional to use diagonal grids for appliqué background quilting. The straight lines balance the curves in the appliqué motifs.

1 To mark a diagonal quilting design, place dots at 1" intervals along the edges of the 10" blocks.

2 Use a long ruler to connect the dots and mark the diagonal lines. Lines on adjacent blocks will connect for an overall design. You can mark parallel diagonal lines in only one direction or in both directions for a lattice grid.

In a four-block quilt, you can use a variation of this technique. Mark the dots at 1" intervals on the blocks and mark the diagonals in one direc-

tion within each block so that they originate in the center of the quilt as shown.

3 Quilt along the lines.

BORDER QUILTING

Here are two ideas for marking the quilting designs on your borders.

- Mark the border quilting lines 1" apart, perpendicular to the quilt edge. To help keep the lines straight, place dots at 1" intervals along the outside edge of the inner borders and on the raw edge of the outer borders. Start marking at the center of each border, and then connect the dots for evenly spaced lines. Mark the corners with diagonal lines as shown to create a "fan" effect.

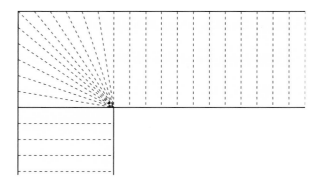

- Connect the dots for diagonal quilting lines. Start in a corner and mark lines parallel to the mitered seam. Change direction when you get to the next corner.

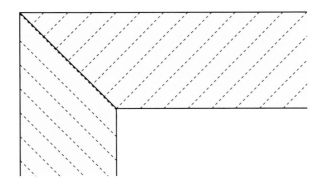

MARKING WITH TAPE

If you don't want to mark the quilt prior to layering and basting, you can use a light-tack masking tape to mark straight lines. Simply place the tape from dot to dot on the layered quilt just before you quilt a line and quilt along the edge of the tape. Peel the tape off with no marks to remove!

Basting the Layers

Before you quilt, baste together the quilt top, batting, and backing. This secures the three layers and keeps the fabrics from slipping during the quilting process.

❶ Press the quilt backing so that it is smooth. Cut the backing at least 4" larger than the quilt top, piecing the fabric together if necessary.

❷ Place the backing, right side down, on a smooth, hard surface. Use masking tape to fasten the corners and sides of the backing to the surface. You can use a floor, but a dining-room table or long "church" table will make it easier to baste.

❸ Place the batting on the backing, carefully smoothing it out. The batting should be several inches larger than the quilt top.

❹ Center the quilt top, right side up, on the batting. Pin the three layers together in several places.

❺ If you plan to hand quilt, baste the three layers together using a long needle and light-colored thread. Start in the center and baste a large X in the center of the quilt. Then, baste parallel grid lines to hold the layers together. The lines should be 3" to 4" apart. The more rows of basting you have, the better your layers will stay together. Finally, baste around the outside edges.

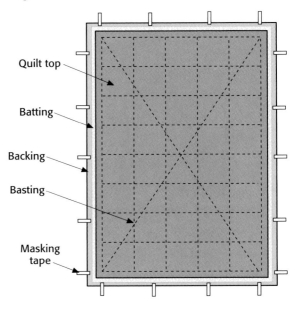

Quilt top
Batting
Backing
Basting
Masking tape

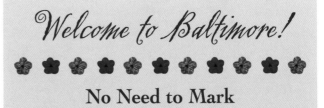

No Need to Mark

You don't need to mark the quilting lines that outline the appliqués, the narrow inner borders, or the sashing strips. Refer to "Quilting Sequence" on page 105.

Nice to Know

You can send the three layers of your quilt to a professional machine quilter. For a fee, many of them will baste the quilt for you.

Hand-Quilting Stitch Technique

Hand-quilting stitches are short running stitches used to sew the three layers of your quilt together.

1. Thread a Between needle with an 18" length of hand-quilting thread and tie a single knot in the long end of the thread. Insert the needle through the top layer of the quilt about 1" from the point where you want to start stitching. Slide the needle under the top and through the batting layer (not through the backing). Bring the needle out at the starting point.

2. Gently tug on the thread until the knot pops through the fabric and becomes buried in the batting. Take a stitch and begin quilting, making small running stitches that go equally through all layers. Take two, three, or four stitches at a time, trying to keep them straight and even.

3. To end a line of quilting, make a single knot approximately ¼" from your quilt top. Take a small backstitch into your quilt, through the top and batting only; tug the knot into the batting and bring the needle out ¾" from your stitches. Clip the thread even with the top and let the end disappear into your quilt.

4. Some quilters use a quilting frame that holds the entire quilt stretched during the quilting process, but a larger number of quilters use a quilting hoop that is more portable. When you place the quilt in the hoop, loosen the outer hoop a bit so that it doesn't distort the quilt.

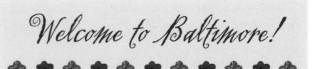

Leave It to the Pros

Some Baltimore quiltmakers love to appliqué but send their quilts to a professional for quilting. Some professional quilters will even bind the quilt for you! What a wonderful feeling it is to have a *finished* quilt returned to you! See "Resources" on page 111 for a reference.

Quilting Sequence

Whether you make a quilt with four blocks, nine blocks, or a full-size quilt, I recommend this sequence for quilting your Baltimore Album quilt.

1. Quilt around the outside edges of all appliqué pieces in the quilt blocks. Place stitches just outside the appliqué edge, stitching through the quilt background, batting, and backing. This outline quilting will accent your designs and make your appliqué pieces puff slightly. This technique is sometimes called quilting in the ditch.

2. Quilt along the inner and outer edges of the narrow inner border of your quilt and any sashing strips. Since your seam allowances should be pressed under the inner border, you should quilt against the resulting ridge. You'll only be quilting through one layer of fabric on the top of the quilt. Be careful to keep this line straight so that the quilt doesn't become distorted.

3. Quilt the background design in the center of the quilt.

4. Quilt around the outside edges of all appliqué pieces in the quilt borders.

5. Quilt the background design in the borders.

Machine Quilting

"By the time I finish this quilt, *I'm* going to be the heirloom!"

Most Baltimore Album appliqué stitchers feel that the only way to quilt a hand-appliquéd album is by hand. However, machine quilting can be a wonderful way to get a quilt finished in your lifetime! I know of some quilters who have mixed both hand and machine methods to finish their quilts.

If you plan to machine quilt, you can employ the marking techniques described in "Marking the Quilting Design" on page 102. Use safety pins or a quilt-tack tool to baste the quilt layers together at 3" to 4" intervals. A lightweight cotton batting or 80/20 blend is easy to handle when machine quilting. The cotton fabric tends to stick to the cotton batting, thus helping to improve your control.

After some practice, you can quilt fairly quickly by machine. Adjust your stitch length to approximately 10 to 12 stitches per inch. Test your machine by stitching on a sample quilt sandwich (two layers of fabric with a scrap of batting between them) to make sure that the thread tension is even on the top and bottom.

STRAIGHT-LINE QUILTING

Use a walking foot or even-feed foot on your machine to stitch straight or slightly curved lines, to outline borders or sashing strips, or to quilt in the ditch. The walking foot helps to ease the top and bottom quilt layers evenly through the machine, creating smooth results.

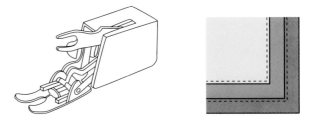

Walking or even-feed foot

FREE-MOTION QUILTING

Machine quilters often use free-motion quilting to fill in the background areas or borders. Use this technique to outline a motif or flower in the fabric or to meander around the appliqués.

Use a darning foot and lower or cover the feed dogs on your machine so that you can freely move the fabric in the direction that you choose. Take a little time to practice and sew a sample before you actually sew on your quilt.

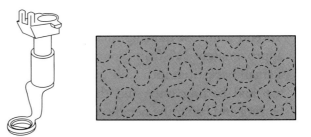

Darning foot

Congratulations! You're ready to finish your Baltimore Album quilt with a hanging sleeve, binding, and a special label. To prepare your quilt for the finishing touches, baste around the edges to securely hold the three layers together. Trim excess threads, batting, and backing even with the front of the quilt. I trim my quilts using a plastic ruler and a rotary cutter, but I always check carefully before I cut!

Hanging Sleeve

If you wish to hang your quilt for display, sew a sleeve to the back of your quilt before you apply the binding. You can insert a rod in this sleeve to display your quilt on the wall.

❶ Measure the top edge of your quilt. Cut a strip or strips to equal this length x 6½" wide. Piece strips together and press the seam open. This strip will make a 3"-wide sleeve.

❷ Turn under ½" twice at each short end of the strip and stitch a narrow hem. Creating a generous hem will ensure that you won't catch the ends of the sleeve in the binding. It also helps to hide the ends of your hanging rod if you don't want to use a decorative rod.

❸ Fold the sleeve lengthwise, wrong sides together, and pin the raw edges to the top of the quilt back. Machine baste ⅛" from the top edge. When you sew the binding to the quilt, the raw edge of the sleeve will be covered.

Fold

Quilt back

❹ After the binding has been added, pin the folded edge of the sleeve to the back of the quilt. Blindstitch the sleeve to the back of the quilt by hand, being careful not to stitch through to the front of the quilt.

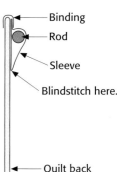

Binding
Rod
Sleeve
Blindstitch here.
Quilt back

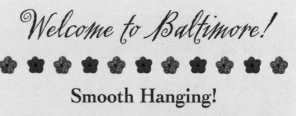

Welcome to Baltimore!

Smooth Hanging!

When you pin the bottom folded edge of the sleeve to the back of the quilt, roll the edge up ¼". This adds a little extra room for the hanging rod and helps the front of the quilt hang smoothly.

Binding

Binding adds the finishing touch to your quilt. Use your border fabric, or an accent fabric that nicely frames your design.

MAKING STRAIGHT-GRAIN BINDING

❶ Use a rotary cutter, mat, and ruler to cut 2" x 42" binding strips. Cut enough strips to go around your entire quilt plus 10".

❷ Sew the strips together using a diagonal seam to create one long strip of binding. To make a diagonal seam, cross and pin the two strip ends at right angles with right sides together. Lay these on a flat surface and imagine the strips as a large letter A. Draw a line across the crossed pieces to cross the A, and then sew along the line. Your seam will be exact, and you can unfold a continuous strip.

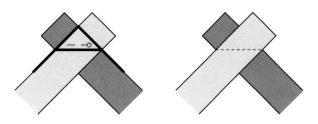

3 Trim the excess fabric, leaving a ¼"-wide seam allowance. Press the seam open to distribute the thickness of the seam.

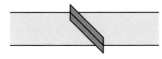

4 Fold the binding strip in half lengthwise, wrong sides together, and press with a hot steam iron.

SEWING BINDING TO THE QUILT

1 Machine baste with a ⅛" seam around the edge of the quilt to securely hold the three layers together. Trim any excess threads, batting, or backing even with the front of the quilt.

2 Starting in the center on a side or bottom of the quilt, align the raw edges of the binding with the raw edges of the quilt. Start sewing 6" from the end of the binding, using a ¼" seam allowance.

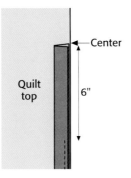

3 To miter the corners of the binding, stop stitching ¼" from the corner and backstitch.

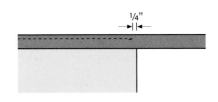

4 Fold the binding diagonally so that it extends straight up from the second edge of the quilt as shown.

5 Fold the binding down even with the second edge of the quilt and pin in place. The fold should be even with the first edge. Start sewing the binding ¼" from the fold, making sure to backstitch. Repeat for the remaining corners. End the stitching about 4" before the starting point.

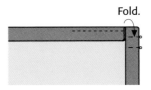

6 To connect the ends of the binding, allow the end to overlap the beginning by 2". Unfold the binding strip and cut the end diagonally, with the shortest end of the diagonal on top, nearest to you. Turn the diagonal edge under ¼" and insert the beginning tail inside the diagonal fold. Continue sewing the binding onto the quilt.

Turn under ¼" on diagonal end.

Tuck end inside.

7 Fold the binding over the edge of the quilt so that it covers the stitching on the back of the quilt. As you fold the corner to the back of the quilt, a folded miter will appear on the front.

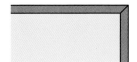

On the back, fold one side first, and then the other, to create a mitered corner.

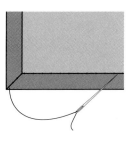

8 Hand stitch the binding to the back of the quilt, using the traditional appliqué stitch. Hand stitch the diagonal folds at the corners.

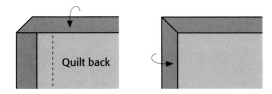

Signing Your Quilt

You've made a very special quilt and now you need to sign it! Here are some suggestions.

- In the tradition of the Baltimore Album quilts, sign your name on the front of your quilt. Use a fine-line permanent marking pen. Write your name in your own handwriting for a personal touch and be sure to include the date. Practice on a scrap of background fabric with freezer paper ironed to the back to keep the fabric stable while you write.

- You can print your name in a fancy font on computer paper. Then use a light box to trace your name on a quilt block before you finish the quilt. It will look great!

- Make a label for the back of your quilt that includes the name of the quilt, your name, and the date. Include information about your quilt, a dedication, or a story about your quilt.

- Design your own label or trace a quilt design. Add your lettering with a permanent marking pen or embroidery stitches and attach the label to your quilt with the traditional appliqué stitch.

> ## Welcome to Baltimore!
>
> ❀ ❀ ❀ ❀ ❀ ❀ ❀ ❀ ❀ ❀
>
> ### The Next Generation
>
> One of my students made a fabric envelope that she stitched to the back of her quilt. She wrote a note to her future grandchildren and placed it in the envelope.

Happy Dance

Wow! You've finished your quilt! Turn on your favorite music, call your best friend, break out the champagne, and do a happy dance. Celebrate!

Appliqué Glossary

Here are some common appliqué terms you may find helpful.

Appliqué: A method of sewing pieces of fabric on top of a larger background fabric piece to create a design.

Appliqué stitch: A small, nearly invisible stitch used to attach appliqué fabric to the background fabric.

Background fabric: A large piece of fabric to which appliqué shapes are stitched.

Basting: Temporarily holding fabric in place by stitching, pinning, or gluing.

Bias: A diagonal line that runs at a 45° angle to the threads in the fabric. Fabric has the greatest amount of stretch on the bias.

Freezer-paper appliqué: A method of preparing appliqué shapes using templates cut from freezer paper.

Fussy cutting: Cutting an appliqué piece from a specific area of a fabric design, such as leaves or flowers.

Glue basting: Using a dab of glue stick to temporarily hold fabric in place.

Hand appliqué: Stitching the appliqués to the background fabric using hand-sewing techniques.

Hand basting: Using a hand-sewing needle, thread, and running stitches to temporarily hold fabric in place.

Layered appliqué: A design with appliqués that overlap other appliquéd pieces.

Needle-turn appliqué: A method of turning the seam allowance of the appliqué pieces under as you sew them to the background fabric.

Pattern overlay: A tracing of the appliqué pattern on template plastic, lightweight interfacing, tracing paper, or acetate. The overlay is then placed over your background fabric to accurately position appliqué pieces.

Pin basting: Using pins to temporarily hold fabric in place.

Seam allowance: The extra fabric outside the finished appliqué shape. The standard appliqué seam allowance is ¼" on all sides of an appliqué piece. Sometimes the directions may call for a skimpy or generous ¼" seam allowance. This means to make your seam allowance just a little narrower or wider than ¼".

Straight grain: The threads that run the length (lengthwise grain) and width (crosswise grain) of the fabric.

Template: An appliqué shape cut from plastic, freezer paper, or cardboard and used as a pattern for tracing a design onto fabric or paper. Cut appliqué templates the finished size of the shape and don't include seam allowances.

Window template: A shape cut into a piece of paper that lets you preview fabric choices or correctly position layered appliqué pieces.

Resources

Appliqué Groups

Baltimore Appliqué Society
PO Box 2457
Ellicott City, MD 21043-2457
www.baltimoreapplique.com

The Appliqué Society
PO Box 89
Sequim, WA 98382-0089
www.theappliquesociety.org

Baltimore Museums

Baltimore Museum of Art
10 Art Museum Dr.
Baltimore, MD 21218-3898
www.artbma.org

Maryland Historical Society
(online exhibit of Baltimore Album Quilts)
201 W. Monument St.
Baltimore, MD 21201-4674
www.mdhs.org

Hand-Quilting Service

Bellwether Dry Goods
Richard and Georgina Fries
PO Box 6
Lothian, MD 20711
410-867-0665
www.bellwetherdrygoods.com

About the Author

Mimi Dietrich has been appliquéing for as long as she can remember! Her first quilt, made for her son Jon in 1974, was a Sunbonnet Sue–Overall Bill quilt with a dimensional hankie in Bill's pocket. One of her latest quilts was an appliquéd quilt for Jon's baby daughter, Julia. Mimi loves having a granddaughter—and sewing pink quilts and smocked dresses!

Mimi has lived in Baltimore all her life and is inspired by the beautiful Baltimore Album appliqué quilts made in her hometown more than 150 years ago. She is a "Founding Mother" of the Village Quilters and the Baltimore Appliqué Society. She teaches a yearlong appliqué class in Baltimore and inspires students to create their own special album quilts. She hopes to inspire you to start—or finish—an album quilt with the patterns, tips, and techniques in this book.

Mimi has published many books with Martingale & Company. Her most recent was *Easy Appliqué Samplers: 20 Designs to Mix and Match* and her very first book, *Happy Endings: Finishing the Edges of Your Quilt*, is still a bestseller.